ANDS

:unono

MERICAN
SAMOA

:wains Atoll

u

Manua
:o Islands

uila :·

Rakahanga o
o Manahiki

:·Danger Atoll

o Nassau Island

o
Suvorov

ISLANDS

SOC.

Palmerston
:oo:

ꝋ Niue

COOK

Aitutaki o
Manuae::: Mitiaro

Atiu o ·:
o Mauke

Rarotonga o

Mangaia o

Rim.

NGA

TROPIC OF
CAPRICORN

Rodolphe Meyer de Schauensee

Ex Libris

SOUTH PACIFIC BIRDS

Delaware Museum of Natural History

Monograph Series No. 3

To Rodolphe
With best wishes
                John
April 18, 1976

SOUTH PACIFIC BIRDS

by John E. duPont

Illustrations by George Sandström

1976

SOUTH PACIFIC BIRDS
by John E. duPont

Library of Congress catalog number: 75-23917

ISBN: 0-913176-04-4

Editorial production and design by *Weidner Associates, Inc.,* Cinnaminson, New Jersey 08077. Manufactured in the United States of America. Color reproductions and printing by Beck Engraving Co., Inc., Philadelphia, Pa.

FOREWORD

Although John duPont and I have been friends for some years, having originally been drawn together through our common interest in the birds of the Philippine Islands, I confess that his work habits still baffle me. Somehow he must have found the secret of the thirty-hour day. As a principal member of the duPont industrial dynasty, his responsibilities in the management of major financial resources might be considered a full-time job by many people. But John has a quality of eager versatility, combined with an uncanny ability to focus on the immediate task at hand, that one cannot help admiring and envying. In indulging his several diverse enthusiasms, he is not content with mere hobby-level pursuits, but has sought to make genuine contributions to the fields of his interests. As an international athletic competitor himself, for example, he has quietly supported facilities for the training of young people in athletics. A boyhood interest in shell-collecting and in bird-watching eventually led to his founding the Delaware Museum of Natural History, now the custodian of some of the most important malacological and ornithological research collections in America.

A bibliophile, John duPont has a magnificent collection of the famous ornithological monographs of the nineteenth century. Although the era of these leather-bound folio volumes with hand-colored plates is now long over, there is no end to the production of new "bird books." At least half of those that have appeared in recent years have had little or no rationale beyond an acknowledgement by commercial publishers that bird books with colored pictures will sell well, to a voracious and largely uncritical market. But in choosing the subject matter for his own first two bird books, John duPont has tried to fill genuine needs. Until the appearance of his *Philippine Birds* in 1971, there had never been a complete set of colored illustrations of the birds of that fascinating archipelago. Nor has there ever been a handbook, illustrated or not, to the particular group of islands characterized as "South Pacific" in the present book.

I suspect the existence of a strong romantic streak in John duPont. The lure of the Pacific islands is legendary, but beyond their languorous climate and their hospitable human inhabitants lurks an intriguing and in some ways unique avifauna. Endemism is rampant on these remote bits of land in a huge and largely empty ocean, and flightless birds have evolved more often among the Pacific islands than anywhere else in the world. All too many Pacific species are either known or suspected to be extinct, or are seriously threatened. John has made a special point of searching for some of these during his field trips, knowing in advance that he was probably doomed to disappointment but unwilling to concede the loss of a species until he had done his personal best to find it.

I need hardly say, then, that much of the information in the present book is rooted in John duPont's own field experience. He has also studied the collections of Pacific birds in all the major museums of North America, as well as in some of those abroad, and has uncovered any number of island records here published for the first time. In writing the text, he has broadened the format used in *Philippine Birds* by adding some ecological and life history notes to the species accounts, thus increasing the potential usefulness of the book.

Comparison of George Sandström's earliest bird paintings in *Philippine Birds* with those in this book clearly demonstrates his impressive growth as an ornithological artist. His illustrations for *South Pacific Birds* should ensure the book's value as a field guide, while the meticulous documentation of nomenclatural and distributional data provides an important reference work for the research ornithologist.

KENNETH C. PARKES
Carnegie Museum of Natural History
Pittsburgh, Pennsylvania
June 1975

INTRODUCTION

The South Pacific is a large expanse of ocean dotted with some of the most beautiful islands in the world. Most of the volcanic islands appeared during the Tertiary Period; some today are just atolls, whereas others rise to elevations of 8000 feet. The resident bird population came primarily from the Australian and Asian stock, with several intrusions over many thousands of years that left behind an ornithological complex of isolated species and subspecies. Man has affected this avifauna by extirpating some populations (directly or through habitat destruction) and by introducing alien species.

This text deals with the Fiji, Tongan, Samoan, Cook, Society, Tuamotu, Marquesas, Austral, Pitcairn, and Henderson Groups. Research has shown some discrepancy and inconsistency in the naming and spelling of place locations in these groups. Consequently, for the citation of localities under "Range," an attempt has been made here to minimize confusion by adhering, as much as possible, to the name and spelling as given in the gazetteers of *Official Standard Names Approved by the U. S. Board on Geographic Names,* prepared in the Office of Geography, Department of the Interior, Washington, D. C. For the convenience of the reader, a list of islands, including obsolete names and alternative spellings that appear in the ornithological literature, will be found in the "List of Island Names," following the main text.

Thirty years have passed since the appearance of Mayr's excellent *Birds of the Southwest Pacific,* which covered an area chiefly west of that in the present book, overlapping only from Fiji to Samoa. Since that time an increase in field explorations and nomenclatorial changes have necessitated a fresh survey of this complex avian fauna. The purpose of this book is to present a ready identification guide to all the known South Pacific birds, with a colored illustration of most species.

The format is as simple as possible. Taxonomy, nomenclature, and species sequence are a composite of Peters' *Check-list* and other standard sources, modified by recent revisions and the author's own studies. A standard English name has been chosen from among those in the most recent publications. A brief description supplements the color plates, and often includes plumages not figured. Original citations are given to scientific names that have been applied to South Pacific birds. The type localities are added in parentheses at the end of each bibliographic reference. In general, only the South Pacific range is given, except for the origin of migrants and strays. Islands from which the birds have been recorded are listed alphabetically within major groups. A brief note about some of the life histories is in the "remarks" section.

The basic material used for research consisted of the field notes and specimens from the Whitney South Sea Expedition and other field notes and specimens in the American Museum of Natural History; specimens in the British Museum (Natural History) and specimens in the United States National Museum of Natural History; the ornithological litera-ture; and the author's notes from his travels in the South Pacific. No comprehensive list of specimens collected by the Whitney Expedition was ever published. For some groups of birds, the island records accu-mulated by this Expedition are reported here for the first time.

All measurements are in millimeters and represent an average of a series. Soft-part colors have been taken from previous works and from labels; in the case of a discrepancy, the author has referred to his own field notes.

ACKNOWLEDGMENTS

I would like to express my deepest appreciation to Dr. Kenneth C. Parkes of the Carnegie Museum of Natural History and to Dr. David M. Niles of the Delaware Museum of Natural History. Both of these gentlemen read early versions of the text and offered invaluable suggestions in the planning and organizing of the book.

I am deeply indebted to His Majesty Taufa'ahaa Tupou IV, K.C.M.G., K.B.E., King of the Kingdom of Tonga, and to His Excellency the late Fiane Mataafa Faumuina Mulinu'u II, C.B.E., formerly Prime Minister of the Independent State of Western Samoa, for their personal help and that of their governments in connection with some of my field research work.

I would like to acknowledge my gratitude to Tofilau Luamanuvae Vaaelua Eti, Cabinet Member of Western Samoa for his gracious hospitality on many occasions.

My thanks are also extended to the following persons for the loan of material, for locality records, and for kindnesses extended to me when I visited their institutions: Mr. Rodolphe Meyer de Schauensee and Dr. Frank B. Gill of the Academy of Natural Sciences of Philadelphia; Dr. Dean Amadon, Mr. John Farrand, Jr., Dr. Wesley E. Lanyon, Mrs. Mary K. LeCroy, and Dr. Lester L. Short of the American Museum of Natural History; Dr. David W. Snow, Dr. Philip J. Burton, and Mr. Ian C. J. Galbraith of the British Museum (Natural History); Dr. Laurence C. Binford of the California Academy of Sciences; Dr. Constantine W. Benson of the Cambridge University Museum; Mr. Melvin A. Traylor of the Chicago Field Museum; Dr. Oscar T. Owre of the University of Miami; Dr. S. Dillon Ripley, Dr. Storrs L. Olson, and Dr. Richard L. Zusi of the United States National Museum; and Dr. Charles G. Sibley of the Yale Peabody Museum.

I express gratitude to my secretary, Mrs. Lillian Moll, for her patience and care in preparing the manuscript for publication.

John E. duPont

CONTENTS

SOUTH PACIFIC BIRDS

ROYAL ALBATROSS   PLATE 1

Diomedea epomophora Lesson, 1825

1825   *Diomedea epomophora* Lesson, Ann. Sci. Nat., **6**:95 (Campbell Island)

Description: Male—all white, wing-coverts mottled with black, primaries black. Female—similar to male but wing-coverts entirely black. Nostrils open forward.
Soft Parts: Bill, upper mandible pink with a black lower edge, lower mandible pink; iris brown; feet fleshy white, webs bluish.
Measurements: Wing ♂ 693, ♀ 671; tail ♂ 215, ♀ 205; bill ♂ 193, ♀ 175; tarsus ♂ 137, ♀ 125.
Range: ? Fiji (one sight record)

Remarks: This bird is a rare straggler to the South Pacific from the Subantarctic. Extreme caution should be used when trying to distinguish it from the very similar Wandering Albatross.

WANDERING ALBATROSS   PLATE 1

Diomedea exulans Linnaeus, 1758

1758   *Diomedea exulans* Linnaeus, Syst. Nat., **1**:132 (Cape of Good Hope)

Description: Similar to the *D. epomophora* and cannot be distinguished with certainty in the field. In the hand, the bill of *D. exulans* has the nostrils opening upward, whereas in *D. epomophora* the nostrils open forward.
Soft Parts: Bill pinkish cream; iris black; feet cream.
Measurements: Wing ♂ 635, ♀ 615; tail ♂ 220, ♀ 210; bill ♂ 170, ♀ 160; tarsus ♂ 115, ♀ 110.
Range: Visits Fiji (one record at sea) and the Marquesas Islands.

Remarks: This bird is a rare visitor to the South Pacific, but it should be looked for at sea.

1

BLACK-BROWED ALBATROSS   PLATE 1

Diomedea melanophris Temminck, 1828

1828   *Diomedea melanophris* Temminck, Pl. Col., livr. 77, pl. 456 (Cape of Good Hope)

Description: Head, neck, rump, upper tail-coverts, and underparts white; a small area before eye and a stripe behind eye blackish; back, wings, and tail black. Underside of wing white with black edges. Immature—darker under wings; cap and nape dusky; bill grayish green.

Soft Parts: Bill yellow with a fine black line at the base of the mandibles; iris brown; feet blue-gray.

Measurements: Wing ♂ 510, ♀ 500; tail ♂ 222, ♀ 210; bill ♂ 107, ♀ 104; tarsus ♂ 80, ♀ 76.

Range: Visits Fiji (one record) and Pitcairn Island from the Subantarctic.

Remarks: This albatross is a bird of the open seas.

LIGHT-MANTLED SOOTY ALBATROSS   PLATE 1

Phoebetria palpebrata (Forster, 1785)

1785   *Diomedea palpebrata* Forster, Mem. Math. Phys. Paris, **10**:571 (47° S. lat. to 71°10′ = 64° S., 38° E.)

Description: Top of head, nape, and mantle pale gray; face dark brown; wings and tail dark gray; breast and belly gray.

Soft Parts: Bill black with blue groove in lower mandible; iris hazel; incomplete eye-ring white; feet pink.

Measurements: Wing ♂ 540, ♀ 518; tail ♂ 296, ♀ 283; bill ♂ 110, ♀ 108; tarsus ♂ 75, ♀ 73.

Range: Visits the Marquesas Islands from the Subantarctic.

Remarks: This albatross is a bird of the open seas.

GIANT PETREL   PLATE 2

Macronectes giganteus (Gmelin, 1789)

1789   *Procellaria gigantea* Gmelin, Syst. Nat., **1**:563 (Staten Island)

Description: Entire bird uniform dark brown with slightly paler margins to the feathers. This species also occurs in a scarcer pale gray phase.
Soft Parts: Bill pale yellowish horn; iris brown; feet dark gray.
Measurements: Wing ♂ 510, ♀ 495; tail ♂ 178, ♀ 175; bill 105; tarsus 88.
Range: Visits the Austral Islands (one record), Fiji, and the Tuamotu Archipelago as a visitor from the Subantarctic region. Its subspecific identity is uncertain.

CAPE PIGEON or PINTADO PETREL   PLATE 2

Daption capense (Linnaeus, 1758)

1758   *Procellaria capensis* Linnaeus, Syst. Nat., **1**:132 (Cape of Good Hope)

Description: Head and neck very dull dark blue-gray; back, rump, and wing-coverts white, feathers tipped with sooty black, giving a spotted appearance; wing primaries dark blackish brown with large white patch at base; tail white with a terminal blackish brown band; chin and throat white with a few brown spots; rest of underparts white.
Soft Parts: Bill black; iris brown; feet black.
Measurements: Wing ♂ 260, ♀ 256; tail ♂ 105, ♀ 100; bill 35; tarsus 42.
Range: Visits the Marquesas Islands (rarely) from the Subantarctic.

TAHITI PETREL   PLATE 2

Pterodroma rostrata rostrata (Peale, 1848)

1848   *Procellaria rostrata* Peale, U. S. Expl. Expd., **8**:296 (Mountains about 6000' on Tahiti, Society Islands)

Description: Head, neck, and all upperparts dark brown; breast, belly, and under tail-coverts white.
Soft Parts: Bill black; iris brown; feet black, upper one third and tarsus flesh color.
Measurements: Wing ♂ 297, ♀ 289; tail ♂ 115, ♀ 116; bill 36; tarsus 48.
Range: This bird breeds on the Marquesas Islands and the Society Islands.

4

PLATE 1

A

B   C

E   D

PLATE 1

SANDSTRÖM

PLATE 2

A GIANT PETREL
   (*Macronectes giganteus*), male—page 3

B TAHITI PETREL
   (*Pterodroma rostrata*), male—page 3

C CAPE PIGEON or PINTADO PETREL
   (*Daption capense*), male—page 3

D PHOENIX PETREL
   (*Pterodroma alba*), male—page 8

E MURPHY'S PETREL
   (*Pterodroma ultima*), male—page 8

A

B

C

D

E

PLATE 2

SANDSTRÖM

PHOENIX PETREL   PLATE 2

Pterodroma alba (Gmelin, 1789)

1789   *Procellaria alba* Gmelin, Syst. Nat., **1**:565 (Turtle and Christmas Islands = Christmas Island)

1848   *Procellaria parvirostris* Peale, U. S. Expl. Expd., **8**:298 (Pukapuka Island, Tuamotu Group)

1902   *Oestrelata wortheni* Rothschild, Bull. Brit. Orn. Cl., **12**:62 (lat. 3° S., long. 118°45′ W., Pacific Ocean)

Description: Head, face, collar on hind neck, and upperparts brownish black; breast and belly white; under tail-coverts white barred with grayish black.

Soft Parts: Bill black; iris blackish; feet black, upper one third and tarsus whitish.

Measurements: Wing ♂ 276, ♀ 276; tail ♂ 112, ♀ 112; bill 27; tarsus 33.

Range: Breeds on Ducie, Henderson Island, the Marquesas Islands, Oeno, Tonga, and the Tuamotu Archipelago. Visits Pitcairn Island, the Samoas, and the Society Islands.

MURPHY'S PETREL   PLATE 2

Pterodroma ultima Murphy, 1949

1949   *Pterodroma ultima* Murphy, Ornith. als bio. Wissenschaft, Festschrift zum 60. Geburtstag von Erwin Stresemann, Heidelberg, p. 89 (Oeno Island, subtropical South Pacific)

Description: Forehead, chin, and throat white mottled with sooty gray; rest of bird sooty gray.

Soft Parts: Bill black; iris brown; feet black, upper one third and tarsus whitish.

Measurements: Wing ♂ 279, ♀ 282; tail ♂ 113, ♀ 113; bill 29; tarsus 38.

Range: Breeds on the Austral Islands, Ducie, Henderson Island, Oeno, and the Tuamotu Archipelago. Visits Pitcairn Island and the Society Islands.

KERMADEC PETREL   PLATE 3

Pterodroma neglecta (Schlegel, 1863)

1863   *Procellaria neglecta* Schlegel, Mus. Pays-Bas, **6**:10 (Sunday Island, Kermadec Group)

Description: This petrel comes in many color phases, varying from almost black to ones with pale gray upperparts and pure white underparts. This species differs from others by having the shaft streaks of the primaries white and the tail more square.
Soft Parts: Bill black; iris brown; feet black, upper one third and tarsus pinkish flesh.
Measurements: Wing ♂ 290, ♀ 289; tail ♂ 100, ♀ 101; bill 30; tarsus 38.
Range: Breeds on the Austral Islands, Ducie, Oeno, and the Tuamotu Archipelago. Visits Henderson Island and Pitcairn Island.

HERALD PETREL   PLATE 3

Pterodroma arminjoniana heraldica (Salvin, 1888)

1888   *Aestrelata heraldica* Salvin, Ibis, p. 357 (Chesterfield Islands)

Description: This petrel has many color phases, with upperparts brownish and underparts whitish; but it usually has the forehead and lores scaled with white, the collar on the hind neck grayish, and the under tail-coverts mottled with white.
Soft Parts: Bill black; iris brown; feet black, upper one third and tarsus whitish.
Measurements: Wing ♂ 278, ♀ 277; tail ♂ 106, ♀ 105; bill 27; tarsus 33.
Range: Breeds on Ducie, Henderson Island, the Marquesas Islands, Oeno, Tonga, and the Tuamotu Archipelago. Visits Pitcairn Island and the Society Islands.

COLLARED PETREL   PLATE 3

Pterodroma leucoptera brevipes (Peale, 1848)

1848   *Procellaria brevipes* Peale, U. S. Expl. Expd., 8:294 (lat. 68° S., long. 95° W.)

Description: Crown, nape, and sides of breast dark sooty gray; back and rump gray; wings and tail sooty black; underparts white.
Soft Parts: Bill black; iris brown; feet black, upper one third and tarsus bluish white.
Measurements: Wing ♂ 218, ♀ 216; tail ♂ 95, ♀ 95; bill 24; tarsus 26.
Range: Breeds on Fiji and the Samoas. Visits the Tuamotu Archipelago.

PLATE 3

A KERMADEC PETREL
   (*Pterodroma neglecta*), female—page 8

B KERMADEC PETREL
   (*Pterodroma neglecta*), male—page 8

C HERALD PETREL
   (*Pterodroma arminjoniana*), male—page 9

D COLLARED PETREL
   (*Pterodroma leucoptera*), male—page 9

E BLACK-WINGED PETREL
   (*Pterodroma axillaris*), male—page 12

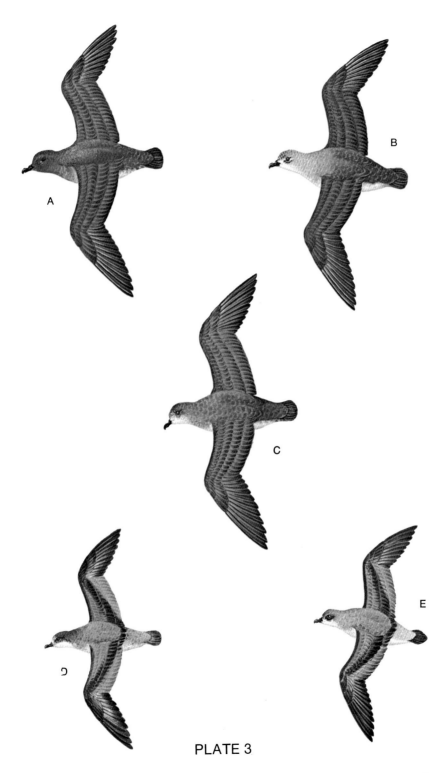

PLATE 3

SANDSTRÖM

BLACK-WINGED PETREL   PLATE 3

Pterodroma axillaris nigripennis (Rothschild, 1893)

1893   *Aestrelata nigripennis* Rothschild, Bull. Brit. Orn. Cl., **1**:57 (Kermadec Islands)

Description: Crown, nape, back, and sides of breast gray; rump whitish; wings and tail sooty black; underparts white.
Soft Parts: Bill black; iris brown; feet black, upper one third and tarsus flesh color.
Measurements: Wing ♂ 227, ♀ 226; tail ♂ 98, ♀ 98; bill 24; tarsus 30.
Range: Visits the Austral Islands, the Marquesas Islands, and the Society Islands from the south.

BULWER'S PETREL   PLATE 4

Bulweria bulwerii (Jardine and Selby, 1828)

1828   *Procellaria bulwerii** Jardine and Selby, Ill. Orn., **2**, pl. 65 (Madeira)

1915   *Bulweria bulweri pacifica* Mathews and Iredale, Ibis, p. 607 (Iwojima, Bonin Islands)

Description: Entire bird sooty brown with a forked tail.
Soft Parts: Bill black; iris brown; feet blackish.
Measurements: Wing ♂ 201, ♀ 195; tail ♂ 107, ♀ 105; bill 21; tarsus 27.
Range: Breeds on the Marquesas Islands. Visits Fiji and the Society Islands.

SOOTY SHEARWATER   PLATE 4

Puffinus griseus (Gmelin, 1789)

1789   *Procellaria grisea* Gmelin, Syst. Nat., **1**:564 (New Zealand)

Description: Entire bird dark brown; the wings and tail darker; the underside of wing contrastingly pale.
Soft Parts: Bill black; iris brown; feet black.
Measurements: Wing ♂ 295, ♀ 293; tail ♂ 88, ♀ 88; bill 41; tarsus 55.
Range: Visits the Marquesas Islands and the Society Islands from New Zealand.

---

*Bulweria macgillivrayi (G. R. Gray, 1859)
   This species is known from only one specimen collected at Ngau, Fiji, in 1855 and differs only by having a slightly larger bill and paler wing-coverts. This may be a possible variant specimen of *bulwerii*.

SLENDER-BILLED SHEARWATER   PLATE 4

Puffinus tenuirostris (Temminck, 1835)

1835   *Procellaria tenuirostris* Temminck, Pl. Col., livr. 99, text to pl. 587 (seas north of Japan and shores of Korea)

Description: Entire bird sooty brown; chin and throat sometimes almost dirty white; rest of underparts pale sooty brown, often with a grayish wash.
Soft Parts: Bill blackish; iris dark brown; feet blackish.
Measurements: Wing ♂ 274, ♀ 271; tail ♂ 81, ♀ 80; bill 33; tarsus 51.
Range: Visits the Samoas and the Tuamotu Archipelago (one record each) from the Northwest Pacific Ocean.

PALE-FOOTED SHEARWATER   PLATE 4

Puffinus carneipes Gould, 1844

1844   *Puffinus carneipes* Gould, Ann. Mag. Nat. Hist., **13**:365 (small islands off Cape Leeuwin, West Australia)

Description: Entire bird dark brown; head, wings, and tail darker.
Soft Parts: Bill flesh color with a black tip; iris brown; feet flesh color.
Measurements: Wing ♂ 326, ♀ 323; tail ♂ 112, ♀ 111; bill 41; tarsus 53.
Range: Visits the Samoas from the Subantarctic region.

WEDGE-TAILED SHEARWATER   PLATE 4

Puffinus pacificus pacificus (Gmelin, 1789)

1789   *Procellaria pacifica* Gmelin, Syst. Nat., **1**:560 (Pacific Ocean = Kermadec Islands)
1925   *Puffinus pacificus whitneyi* Lowe, Bull. Brit. Orn. Cl., **45**:106 (Kandavu Island, Fiji)

Description: Upperparts dark brown, with wings and tail darker; face, chin, and throat gray-brown; rest of underparts brown with a grayish cast. A scarce pale gray-white bellied phase also may be found.
Soft Parts: Bill dark blue-black; iris brown; feet pale flesh color.
Measurements: Wing ♂ 309, ♀ 308; tail ♂ 136, ♀ 137; bill 40; tarsus 50.
Range: Breeds on the Austral Islands, Fiji, Henderson Island, the Marquesas Islands, the Samoas, the Society Islands, Tonga, and the Tuamotu Archipelago.

PLATE 4

PLATE 4

SANDSTRÖM

CHRISTMAS SHEARWATER   PLATE 4

Puffinus nativitatis Streets, 1877

1877   *Puffinus (Nectris) nativitatis* Streets, Bull. U. S. Nat. Mus., 7:29 (Christmas Island, Pacific Ocean)

Description: A small, dark brown bird with the wings and tail somewhat darker.
Soft Parts: Bill black; iris brown; feet black.
Measurements: Wing ♂ 249, ♀ 245; tail ♂ 95, ♀ 95; bill 32; tarsus 44.
Range: Breeds on the Austral Islands, the Marquesas Islands, Oeno, and the Tuamotu Archipelago. Visits the Cook Islands, Ducie, Henderson Island, Pitcairn Island, and the Society Islands.

LITTLE SHEARWATER   PLATE 5

Puffinus assimilis assimilis Gould, 1838

1838   *Puffinus assimilis* Gould, Syn. Bds. Austr., pt. 4, app. 7 (New South Wales = Norfolk Island)

Description: Upperparts very dark gray with a bluish cast in some light; underparts white.
Soft Parts: Bill black; iris brown; feet bluish.
Measurements: Wing ♂ 188, ♀ 184; tail ♂ 73, ♀ 71; bill 29; tarsus 38.
Range: Visits the Austral Islands and the Marquesas Islands from the Subantarctic region.

AUDUBON'S SHEARWATER   PLATE 5

Puffinus lherminieri polynesiae Murphy, 1927

1927   *Puffinus lherminieri polynesiae* Murphy, Am. Mus. Novit., 276:8 (Tahiti, Society Islands)

Description: All upperparts and underparts sooty black, with wing primaries and tail somewhat darker; underparts white.
Soft Parts: Bill black; iris dark brown; feet blackish.
Measurements: Wing ♂ 203, ♀ 202; tail ♂ 83, ♀ 82; bill 29; tarsus 30.
Range: Breeds on Fiji, the Marquesas Islands, the Samoas, the Society Islands, and the Tuamotu Archipelago. Visits Tonga.

WHITE-BELLIED STORM-PETREL   PLATE 5

Fregetta grallaria titan Murphy, 1928

1928 *Fregetta grallaria titan* Murphy, Am. Mus. Novit., 322:4 (Rapa Island, Austral Group, South Pacific)

Description: Upperparts sooty black, with feathers of back having whitish borders; rump white; wings and tail dull black; chin, throat, and under tail-coverts sooty black; breast, belly, and a patch under the wings white.

Soft Parts: Bill black; iris brown; feet black.

Measurements: Wing ♂ 181, ♀ 184; tail ♂ 82, ♀ 83; bill 15; tarsus 40.

Range: Breeds on the Austral Islands (Rapa). Visits the Marquesas Islands and the Society Islands.

Fregetta grallaria grallaria (Vieillot, 1817)

1817 *Procellaria grallaria* Vieillot, Nouv. Dict. d'Hist. Nat., **25**:418 (Juan Fernandez = New South Wales)

1848 *Thalassidroma lineata* Peale, U. S. Expl. Expd., **8**:293 (Upolu, Samoan Islands)

Description: Differs from *F. g. titan* by being smaller. A female collected in the Marquesas measured as follows: wing 165; tail 73; bill 14; tarsus 38.

Range: Marquesas Islands (Ua Pu) (once)
Western Samoa (Upolu) (three old records)
This race may be a rare straggler to the South Pacific from the southern waters.

BLACK-BELLIED STORM-PETREL   PLATE 5

Fregetta tropica (Gould, 1844)

1844 *Thalassidroma tropica* Gould, Ann. Mag. Nat. Hist., **13**:366 (Atlantic Ocean in lat. 33° N., long. 18°6′ W.)

1848 *Thalassidroma lineata* Peale, U. S. Expl. Expd., **8**:293 (Upolu Island, Samoa)

Description: Upperparts sooty black; rump white; wings and tail dull black; chin and throat white with sooty tips to feathers; lower throat and breast sooty black; belly and flanks white, with a sooty black stripe down the center of the belly, varying in width.

Soft Parts: Bill black; iris brown; feet black.
Measurements: Wing ♂ 160, ♀ 163; tail ♂ 72, ♀ 74; bill 15; tarsus 41.
Range: Visits the Marquesas Islands and the Samoas from the Northern Hemisphere.

WHITE-THROATED STORM-PETREL   PLATE 5

Nesofregetta albigularis (Finsch, 1877)

1877 *Procellaria albigularis* Finsch, Proc. Zool. Soc. London, p. 722 (Kandavu, Fiji Islands)
1879 *Fregetta moestissima* Salvin, Proc. Zool. Soc. London, p. 130 (Samoan Islands)

Description: Upperparts, wings, and deeply forked tail sooty black; rump white; underparts white with a sooty brown breast band.
Soft Parts: Bill black; iris brown; feet black.
Measurements: Wing ♂ 186, ♀ 183; tail ♂ 96, ♀ 95; bill 16; tarsus 42.
Range: Breeds on Fiji, the Marquesas Islands, and the Samoas. Visits the Society Islands and the Tuamotu Archipelago.

LEACH'S STORM-PETREL   PLATE 5

Oceanodroma leucorhoa (Vieillot, 1817)

1817 *Procellaria leucorhoa* Vieillot, Nouv. Dict. d'Hist. Nat., **25**:422 (maritime parts of Picardy)

Description: Upperparts sooty brown, rump somewhat paler; wing primaries and tail dull black; underparts sooty brown.
Soft Parts: Bill black; iris brown; feet black.
Measurements: Wing ♂ 150, ♀ 152; tail ♂ 75, ♀ 75; bill 15; tarsus 22.
Range: Visits the Marquesas Islands (rarely). Subspecific identity uncertain.

PHAETHONTIDAE   TROPICBIRDS

RED-BILLED TROPICBIRD   PLATE 6

Phaethon aethereus mesonauta Peters, 1930

1930 *Phaethon aethereus mesonauta* Peters, Occ. Papers Boston Soc. Nat. His., **5**:261 (Swan Key, Almirante Bay, Panama)

Description: Entire bird white with upperparts barred with black; long white tail streamers. Immature—similar to adults but have a black stripe that runs from the eyes and joins behind the crown.
Soft Parts: Bill red (yellow bills in immatures); iris brown; feet yellowish flesh color, plantar surface gray.
Measurements: Wing ♂ 290, ♀ 285; tail 105, streamers 440; bill 60; tarsus 25.
Range: Breeds on the Marquesas Islands. Visits Fiji, the ?Samoas, and the Tuamotu Archipelago.

RED-TAILED TROPICBIRD   PLATE 6

Phaethon rubricauda melanorhynchos Gmelin, 1789

1789   *Phaeton* (sic) *melanorhynchos* Gmelin, Syst. Nat., **1**:582 (Turtle and Palmerston Islands)

Description: Entire bird white, with a black eye stripe; long red tail streamers. Immature—similar to adults but has black barring on the upperparts.
Soft Parts: Bill red (black to orange in immatures); iris brown; feet blue-black.
Measurements: Wing ♂ 345, ♀ 338; tail 97, streamers 450; bill 65; tarsus 26.
Range: Breeds on the Austral Islands, the Cook Islands, Ducie, Fiji, Henderson Island, the Marquesas Islands, Oeno, Pitcairn Island, the Samoas, the Society Islands, Tonga, and the Tuamotu Archipelago.

WHITE-TAILED TROPICBIRD   PLATE 6

Phaethon lepturus dorotheae Mathews, 1913

1913   *Phaethon lepturus dorotheae* Mathews, Austr. Av. Rec., **2**:7 (Queensland)

Description: All white except for a stripe through the eye and outer primaries; a bar on the base of the wing; and the flanks, which are black. Immature—barred black and white on upperparts.

Soft Parts: Bill greenish yellow to orange-yellow, base gray; iris dark brown; legs pinkish; feet black.
Measurements: Wing ♂ 270, ♀ 266; tail 135, streamers 410; bill 53; tarsus 20.
Range: Breeds on the Austral Islands, Fiji, the Marquesas Islands, the Samoas, the Society Islands, Tonga, and the Tuamotu Archipelago. Visits the Cook Islands.

Remarks: This bird is usually found around steep cliffs; however, it also may be seen far at sea.

SULIDAE   BOOBIES

MASKED BOOBY   PLATE 6

Sula dactylatra personata Gould, 1846

1846   *Sula personata* Gould, Proc. Zool. Soc. London, p. 21 (north and northeast coasts of Australia = Raine Island, north Queensland)

Description: All white except for wings and tail, which are dark brown. Immature—differs by having head, throat, and mantle dark brown.
Soft Parts: Bill, male yellow, female pinkish or greenish; face blue-black; iris yellow; feet olive-brown. Immature—bill brown; feet black.
Measurements: Wing ♂ 445, ♀ 436; tail ♂ 189, ♀ 186; bill 104; tarsus 55.
Range: Breeds on Ducie, Fiji, Henderson Island, Oeno, the Samoas, and the Tuamotu Archipelago. Visits the Cook Islands, the Marquesas Islands, Pitcairn Island, and the Society Islands.

Remarks: This bird is usually found on uninhabited islands where there are trees. It can often be seen flying over the ocean.

BROWN BOOBY   PLATE 6

Sula leucogaster plotus (Forster, 1844)

1844   *Pelecanus Plotus* Forster, Descr. Anim., ed. Licht., p. 278 (near New Caledonia)

Description: Head, neck, and upperparts brown; underparts white. Immature—all brown with yellow legs.

Soft Parts: Bill mainly gray; base of bill and naked skin of face and throat blue in males, yellow-green in females. Feet greenish yellow in males, yellow in females. Immature—bill greenish white; face skin and feet greenish yellow.

Measurements: Wing ♂ 400, ♀ 390; tail ♂ 200, ♀ 196; bill 110; tarsus 41.

Range: Breeds on the Austral Islands, Fiji, the Marquesas Islands, the Society Islands, Tonga, and the Tuamotu Archipelago. Visits the Cook Islands, Henderson Island, Pitcairn Island, and the Samoas.

Remarks: This species likes islands where there are lots of rocky cliffs. It also likes uninhabited islands and often flies out to investigate approaching boats.

RED-FOOTED BOOBY   PLATE 6

Sula sula rubripes Gould, 1838

1838   *Sula rubripes* Gould, Syn. Bds. Austr., pt. 4, app. 7 (New South Wales = Raine Island, northern Queensland)

Description: White phase—all white (head washed with yellow) except for primaries and most of secondaries, which are black. Dark phase—all brown. Various intermediate steps exist. Immature—like dark phase adult but feet yellow, not red.

Soft Parts: Bill blue with brown tip and red base; face and throat bluish; iris brown; feet red.

Measurements: Wing ♂ 390, ♀ 375; tail ♂ 220, ♀ 215; bill 78; tarsus 36.

Range: Breeds on the Austral Islands, Fiji, the Marquesas Islands, Oeno, the Samoas, the Society Islands, and the Tuamotu Archipelago. Visits the Cook Islands, Ducie, Henderson Island, Pitcairn Island, and Tonga.

Remarks: This bird of the ocean is usually found around uninhabited islands, especially those with trees.

PLATE 5

A

B

C

D

E

F

PLATE 5

SANDSTRÖM

PLATE 6

PLATE 6

GREATER FRIGATEBIRD   PLATE 6

Fregata minor palmerstoni (Gmelin, 1789)

1789   *Pelecanus Palmerstoni* Gmelin, Syst. Nat., **1**:573 (Palmerston Island, Pacific Ocean)

Description: Male—upperparts dark brown-black; wing-coverts buffy brown; underparts brown-black. Female—similar but has throat and breast white. Immature—head whitish or rufous; bill and throat blue-gray; feet white. Otherwise similar to adult female.

Soft Parts: Bill, male black, female red; throat pouch in male red; iris dark brown; feet, male blackish brown, female pink.

Measurements: Wing ♂ 551, ♀ 590; tail ♂ 400, ♀ 405; bill ♂ 95, ♀ 115; tarsus ♂ 14, ♀ 15.

Range: Breeds on the Marquesas Islands, Oeno, the Society Islands, and the Tuamotu Archipelago. Visits the Austral Islands, the Cook Islands, Ducie, Fiji, Henderson Island, Pitcairn Island, the Samoas, and Tonga.

Remarks: This is a bird of the ocean, most commonly found soaring in the vicinity of islands with cliffs.

LESSER FRIGATEBIRD   PLATE 6

Fregata ariel (G. R. Gray, 1845)

1845   *Atagen* (sic) *Ariel* G. R. Gray, Gen. Bds., **3**, pl. 185 (Raine Island, north Queensland)

Description: Male—all black with a purplish green gloss on the head and neck; flanks white. Female—brown-black except for white collar, flanks, and breast. Immature—head whitish or rufous; bill and feet bluish white. Otherwise similar to adult female.

Soft Parts: Male—bill gray; throat pouch red; iris brown; feet black. Female—bill pink; iris brown; feet pink to red.

Measurements: Wing ♂ 515, ♀ 530; tail 335; bill 88; tarsus 15.

Range: Breeds on Fiji, the Marquesas Islands, the Society Islands, Tonga, and the Tuamotu Archipelago. Visits the Samoas.

Remarks: This bird is commonly found around islands, especially those with cliffs, as it often rides the air currents.

REEF HERON   **PLATE 7**

Egretta sacra sacra (Gmelin, 1789)

1789   *Ardea sacra* Gmelin, Syst. Nat., **1**:640 (Tahiti, Society Islands)

Description: This species is found in three color phases: gray phase—forehead and crown dark blue-gray, neck dark brownish blue, elongated feathers of the back dark blue-gray, tail and wings dark brown, a white stripe from chin part way down the neck, underparts dull gray; white phase—specimens pure white; mottled phase—specimens mottled gray and white.

Soft Parts: Gray phase—bill brown, face greenish yellow, iris yellow, legs and feet yellowish green; white phase—bill yellow, otherwise as in gray phase.

Measurements: Wing ♂ 272, ♀ 260; tail 90; bill 84; tarsus 75.

Range: American Samoa (Manua Islands, Ofu, Olosega, Rose Island, Tutuila)

Austral Islands (Raevavae, Rimatara, Rurutu, Tubuai)

Cook Islands (Rarotonga)

Fiji (Avea, Fulanga, Kambara, Kandavu, Komo, Lakemba, Mango, Marambo, Matuku, Mbatiki, Moala, Mothe, Namuka-I-Lau, Nayau, Nggele Levu, Thikombia, Thithia, Totoya, Vanuambalavu, Vanuavatu, Vatanua, Vatoa, Vatulele, Viti Levu, Wakaya)

Marquesas Islands (Eiao, Fatu Hiva, Fatu Huku, Hiva Oa, Nuku Hiva, Ua Huka, Ua Pu)

Society Islands (Bora-Bora, Huahine, Maiao, Moorea, Mopelia, Raiatea, Scilly, Tahiti, Tetiaroa)

Tonga (Fonuaika, Toku, Vavau)

Tuamotu Archipelago (Ahe, Ahunui, Apataki, Aratika, Faaite, Fakahina, Fakarava, Hao, Hiti, Katiu, Kauehi, Kaukura, Magareva, Makatea, Makemo, Manihi, Marutea, Matahiva, Maturei-Vavao, Mureia, Niau, Nihiru, Rangiroa, Raraka, Raroia, Taenga, Tahanea, Taiaro, Takaroa, Takume, Tenararo, Tenaruga, Tikehau, Timoe Atoll, Toau, Tuanake, Vanavana)

Western Samoa (Apolima, Savaii, Upolu)

Remarks: A common bird of the reefs, it can easily be found feeding in the tide pools.

GREEN HERON   PLATE 7

Butorides striatus diminutus Mayr, 1940

1940   *Butorides striatus diminutus* Mayr, Am. Mus. Novit., 1056:6 (Lomlom Island, Reef Islands)

Description: Top of head and plume dark greenish black; back, wings, and tail dark grayish green; chin and throat whitish with pale spots; rest of underparts gray washed with ochre.
Soft Parts: Bill, upper mandible black, lower mandible yellow; iris yellow; feet greenish yellow.
Measurements: Wing ♂ 183, ♀ 182; tail ♂ 65, ♀ 63; bill 65; tarsus 49.
Range: Fiji (Kandavu, Ngau, Taveuni, Vanuambalavu, Viti Levu)

Butorides striatus patruelis (Peale, 1848)

1848   *Ardea patruelis* Peale, U. S. Expl. Expd., **8**:216 (Tahiti)

Description: Differs from *B. s. diminutus* by lacking the blackish spots in the middle of the throat; underparts more rufous.
Range: Society Islands (Tahiti)

Remarks: A shy bird of the freshwater marshes, it is most active during the early morning hours. Its coloration often makes it most difficult to find.

ANATIDAE   DUCKS

GRAY DUCK   PLATE 7

Anas superciliosa pelewensis Hartlaub and Finsch, 1872

1872   *Anas superciliosa* var. *pelewensis* Hartlaub and Finsch, Proc. Zool. Soc. London, p. 108 (Pelew Islands)

Description: All brown with pale margins to feathers except for a buffy stripe above eye and loral patch; speculum green bordered with black; chin and throat buffy; underwing white.
Soft Parts: Bill blackish; iris brown; feet brownish.
Measurements: Wing ♂ 240, ♀ 226; tail 80; bill 44; tarsus 36.
Range: American Samoa (Aunuu, Tutuila)
           Austral Islands (Rapa, Rimatara, Tubuai)
           Cook Islands (Rarotonga)

Fiji (Kandavu, Mango, Matathawa Levu, Mothe, Ngau, Oneata, Ono-I-Lau, Taveuni, Viti Levu)
Society Islands (Bora-Bora, Huahine, Maiao, Moorea, Raiatea, Tahiti)
Tonga (Fonualei, Niuafoo, Nomuka, Tongatapu, Vavau)
Western Samoa (Savaii, Upolu)

Remarks: This common, widespread duck of the Pacific may be found on streams, rivers, and small lakes. It usually travels in groups of two to 10 and is not shy.

NORTHERN PINTAIL   PLATE 7

Anas acuta Linnaeus, 1758

1758   *Anas acuta* Linnaeus, Syst. Nat., **1**:126 (Europe = Sweden)

Description: Male—head and neck brown with a white line on the side of the neck; mantle and sides gray with fine black bars; back and rump gray; tail black; wings gray with a bronze speculum; scapulars black with light buffy edges; breast and belly white; flanks creamy; under tail-coverts black. Female—above, brown with black specks; below, buffy with black spots on breast; speculum brownish.
Soft Parts: Bill bluish; iris brown; feet gray.
Measurements: Wing ♂ 265, ♀ 245; tail ♂ 190, ♀ 100; bill 49; tarsus 41.
Range: Marquesas Islands (Hiva Oa)
Society Islands (Moorea, Tahiti)
Tonga (Fonualei)

Remarks: This bird breeds in Europe, Asia, and North America. It is migratory and is a rare visitor to the South Pacific. It occasionally appears on freshwater lakes.

NORTHERN SHOVELER   PLATE 7

Anas clypeata Linnaeus, 1758

1758   *Anas clypeata* Linnaeus, Syst. Nat., **1**:124 (coasts of Europe = southern Sweden)

Description: Male—head green; back black; tail black and white; wings gray with a green speculum; scapulars blue and white; breast white; belly chestnut; under tail-coverts black. Female—dull buffy brown with black flecks; green speculum; pale eye stripe.

Soft Parts: Bill black; iris yellow; feet orange.
Measurements: Wing ♂ 245, ♀ 220; tail 79; bill 64; tarsus 35.
Range: Tuamotu Archipelago (Kauehi)

Remarks: This bird breeds in Europe, Asia, and North America. It is migratory and is a rare straggler to the South Pacific.

ACCIPITRIDAE   HAWKS

FIJI GOSHAWK   PLATE 8

Accipiter rufitorques (Peale, 1848)

1848   *Aster rufitorques* Peale, U. S. Expl. Expd., **8**:68 (Fiji Islands)

Description: Top of head gray; collar vinaceous; back, wings, rump, and tail gray; chin and upper throat whitish gray, rest of underparts vinaceous. Immature—upperparts dark brown, feathers with buff margins; underparts white with dark brown streaks; thighs washed with rufous.
Soft Parts: Bill black; iris yellow; feet yellowish.
Measurements: Wing ♂ 220, ♀ 235; tail ♂ 148, ♀ 172; bill ♂ 24, ♀ 29; tarsus ♂ 48, ♀ 59.
Range: Fiji (Avea, Kandavu, Koro, Maiao, Matuka, Matuku, Mbengga, Moala, Nathula, Naviti, Ngau, Ovalau, Rambi, Taveuni, Thithia, Totoya, Vanua Levu, Vanuambalavu, Viti Levu, Waya, Yanutha)

Remarks: A bird of the lowlands, it may be found in open cultivated areas as well as in the dense rain forests. It is not shy.

SWAMP HARRIER   PLATE 8

Circus approximans approximans Peale, 1848

1848   *Circus approximans* Peale, U. S. Expl. Expd., **8**:64 (Mathuata, Venua Levu, Fiji Islands)

Description: Upperparts dark brown with pale margins to feathers; rump and tail very pale brown; underparts rufous-brown feathers with black shaft streaks. Immature—dark brown, unstreaked.
Soft Parts: Bill black; cere yellow; iris yellow; feet yellow.
Measurements: Wing ♂ 403, ♀ 423; tail ♂ 218, ♀ 230; bill 34; tarsus 90.
Range: Fiji (Kandavu, Maiatho, Makongai, Mothe, Naitaumba, Oneata, Taveuni, Thikombia, Viti Levu, Yasawa)
Society Islands (Bora-Bora, Moorea, Raiatea, Tahiti, Tetiaroa)
Tonga (Ata, Tofua)

Remarks: This is a bird of the open lands. It may range from seacoast to mountain tops but is most commonly seen soaring around large hills.

FALCONIDAE   FALCONS

PEREGRINE FALCON   PLATE 8

Falco peregrinus nesiotes Mayr, 1941

1941   *Falco peregrinus nesiotes* Mayr, Am. Mus. Novit., 1133:2 (Tanna Island, New Hebrides)

Description: Top of head, face, and hind neck black; back, rump, and tail dark blue-gray mottled with black; primaries black; chin white; throat and upper breast pale rufous with black streaks; lower breast and belly rufous spotted and streaked with black.
Soft Parts: Bill bluish with black tip; cere yellow; iris brown; feet orange-yellow.
Measurements: Wing ♂ 290, ♀ 310; tail ♂ 132, ♀ 160; bill ♂ 20, ♀ 24; tarsus ♂ 45, ♀ 47.
Range: Fiji (Ovalau, Taveuni, Vanua Levu, Viti Levu, Wakaya)
Western Samoa (Savaii)

Remarks: This is a bird of the mountain cliffs and rain forests, where it can be seen soaring and darting for food. The South Pacific population remains about the same and seems to be in little danger from pesticides and human encroachment.

PLATE 7

A GRAY DUCK
   (*Anas superciliosa*), male—page 28

B NORTHERN PINTAIL
   (*Anas acuta*), male—page 29

C NORTHERN PINTAIL
   (*Anas acuta*), female—page 29

D NORTHERN SHOVELER
   (*Anas clypeata*), male—page 29

E NORTHERN SHOVELER
   (*Anas clypeata*), female—page 29

F REEF HERON—Gray Phase
   (*Egretta sacra*), male—page 27

G REEF HERON—White Phase
   (*Egretta sacra*), male—page 27

H GREEN HERON
   (*Butorides striatus*), male—page 28

PLATE 7

SANDSTRÖM

PLATE 8

A

B

C

D

E

F

PLATE 8

SANDSTRÖM

36

PLATE 9

A BARRED-WING RAIL
(*Nesoclopeus poecilopterus*), male—page 39

B BANDED RAIL
(*Gallirallus philippensis goodsoni*), male—page 39

C HENDERSON ISLAND RAIL
(*Porzana atra*), male—page 41

D SOOTY RAIL
(*Porzana tabuensis*), male—page 41

E WHITE-BROWED RAIL
(*Poliolimnas cinereus*), male—page 42

F PURPLE SWAMPHEN
(*Porphyrio porphyrio samoensis*), male—page 43

G SAMOAN WOOD RAIL
(*Pareudiastes pacificus*)—page 43

PLATE 9

NIUAFO'OU MEGAPODE   PLATE 8

Megapodius pritchardii G. R. Gray, 1864

1864   *Megapodius Pritchardii* G. R. Gray, Ann. Mag. Nat. Hist., **14**:378 (Nina Fou = Nivafo'ou, "Friendly Islands")

1871   *Megapodius huttoni* Buller, Trans. New Zealand Inst., **3**:15 ("Friendly Islands")

Description: Upper back and top of head dark gray; lower back, rump, and wings rufous-brown; wings have a concealed white patch; tail grayish brown with the basal half whitish; throat and breast dark gray; belly pale gray. Immature—duller and lacks the white in the wing. Juvenile—brown, barred with black on back and wings.

Soft Parts: Bill yellow; iris brown; feet yellowish red.

Measurements: Wing 188; tail 74; bill 26; tarsus 54.

Range: Tonga (Niuafoo; introduced on Tafalu in 1968)

Remarks: This megapode, like others of its family, burrows to lay its eggs. The tunnel is 1 to 2 meters long and is placed in volcanic ash near the rim of a crater. Birds are most commonly found on the wooded slopes of a volcano. In 1968, six adults and three immatures were released on Tafalu Island.

JUNGLE FOWL   PLATE 8

Gallus gallus gallus (Linnaeus, 1758)

1758   *Phasianus gallus* Linnaeus, Syst. Nat., **1**:158 (Pulau Condor, off mouth of Mekong River)

1854   *Gallus tahitensis* Hartlaub, Journ. f. Orn., **2**:169 (Tahiti)

1858   *Gallus tahiticus* Cassin, U. S. Expl. Expd., **8**:289 (Tahiti)

Description: Male—head mostly bare red skin; neck has elongated, glossy, reddish orange feathers; back and wing-coverts glossy maroon; rump has elongated, glossy, deep red-orange feathers; wings brown and glossy green; tail black with green gloss; all underparts dull black. Female—mostly dull brown with fine black streaks; neck feathers black with golden yellow margins.

Soft Parts: Bill, upper mandible dark brown, lower mandible light brown; iris orange-red; feet yellowish gray.

Measurements: Wing ♂ 240, ♀ 200; tail ♂ 500, ♀ 130; bill 21; tarsus 78.

Range: This bird was introduced from Asia on most islands throughout the South Pacific, prior to their discovery by European explorers. On most of the larger islands it has returned to the feral state, where it has become quite common yet remains elusive. Its common, chickenlike call makes it very easy to find in the deep forest. Birds of the Pacific Islands are highly variable in color, reflecting introduction of various domesticated European stocks.

RALLIDAE   RAILS

BARRED-WING RAIL   PLATE 9

Nesoclopeus poecilopterus (Hartlaub, 1866)

1866   *Rallina poeciloptera* Hartlaub, Ibis, p. 171 (Viti Levu, Fiji Islands)

Description: Top of head rufous gray-brown, becoming more rufous on hind neck; rest of upperparts rufous brown; wings rufous with black bars; chin and throat whitish; face, sides of neck and breast gray; belly dark gray, feathers slightly tipped with pale gray; flanks and under tail-coverts dark blackish brown.

Soft Parts: Bill yellow, orange at base; iris light brown; feet yellowish.

Measurements: Six specimens = wing 170; tail 83; bill 50; tarsus 65.

Range: Fiji (Ovalau, Viti Levu)

Remarks: This bird may be extinct as it has not been positively recorded during the 20th century; the last specimen was collected during the 1870's. This species was reported to inhabit lowland swamps.

BANDED RAIL   PLATE 9

Gallirallus philippensis goodsoni (Mathews, 1911)

1911   *Eulabeornis philippensis goodsoni* Mathews, Bds. Austr., **1**:197 (Upolu, Samoa)

Description: Forehead and crown brown streaked with black; lores, malar stripe, and hind neck chestnut; stripe above lores and above and behind eye grayish white; upper back gray-black finely barred with white; mantle and rump blackish green with white spots; primaries dark brown with rufous and white spots; chin pale gray; throat gray; rest of underparts barred with black and white; breast sometimes with a faint pale chestnut breast band. Immature—similar to adult but duller and chestnut on head not so extensive.

Soft Parts: Bill, upper mandible brown, lower mandible horn; iris red (red-brown in young birds); feet flesh color.

Measurements: Wing ♂ 150, ♀ 146; tail ♂ 65, ♀ 63; bill 34; tarsus 51.

Range: American Samoa (Manua Islands, Ofu, Olosega, Tau, Tutuila) Western Samoa (Savaii, Upolu)

Gallirallus philippensis sethsmithi (Mathews, 1911)

1911 *Eulabeornis philippensis sethsmithi* Mathews, Bds. Austr., **1**:197 (Ovalau, Fiji Islands)

Description: Differs from *G. p. goodsoni* by having the crown more heavily striped; chestnut of the nape darker and more extensive; narrower white bars on the upper back, giving a darker appearance; and the underparts more finely barred with black.

Range: Fiji (Aiwa, Kandavu, Mango, Moengava, Namenalala, Navandra, Oneata, Ovalau, Viti Levu, Voini, Wakaya) Rotuma

Gallirallus philippensis ecaudata (J. F. Miller, 1783)

1783 *Rallus ecaudata* J. F. Miller, Icon. Anim., pl. 47 ("Otaheitee"; error = Nomuka, Tonga group)
1852 *Rallus Forsteri* Hartlaub, Arch. f. Natürg., **18**:136 (Tonga Islands)
1867 *Rallus hypoleucus* Hartlaub and Finsch, Beitr. Fauna Cent., Orn., p. 163 (Tonga)

Description: Differs from *G. p. goodsoni* by having the chestnut of the crown, nape, and malar stripe paler and the underparts not so heavily barred.

Range: Niue
Tonga (Ava, Foa, Fonualei, Mango, Moungaone, Niuafoo, Niuatoputapu, Nomuka, Ofolanga, Oua, Telekitonga, Tonumea, Tungua)

Remarks: This is a common bird of the open grassy areas, often found around airports and cow pastures and seen darting across roads. On some of the more populated islands and around towns, this bird becomes quite tame to the point where it may be observed feeding with the local chickens.

TAHITI RAIL

Gallirallus pacificus (Gmelin, 1789)

1789   *Rallus pacificus* Gmelin, Syst. Nat., **1**:717 (Tahiti)

Remarks: This rail is known only from a painting by Forster, made during Captain Cook's second voyage (1773 or 1774 [see Lysaght, 1959]). It is shown as black above with white barring, a white eyebrow, white underparts, a red bill, and pink-red legs. It may have been a Tahitian representative of the *Rallus* (or *Gallirallus*) *philippensis* group, but if such a bird really existed on Tahiti, it did not closely resemble any known species. It must be considered hypothetical.

HENDERSON ISLAND RAIL   PLATE 9

Porzana atra North, 1908

1908   *Porzana atra* North, Rec. Austral. Mus., **7**:31 (Henderson Island)
1913   *Porzana murrayi* Ogilvie-Grant, Bull. Brit. Orn. Cl., **31**:61 (Henderson Island)

Description: Entire bird blackish. Immature—grayer below, with black legs.
Soft Parts: Bill black, greenish at base; iris red; feet orange-red.
Measurements: Wing ♂ 84, ♀ 82; tail ♂ 40, ♀ 40; bill ♂ 23, ♀ 21; tarsus ♂ 36, ♀ 34.
Range: Henderson Island

Remarks: This secretive, flightless rail is usually found on the forest floor.

SOOTY RAIL   PLATE 9

Porzana tabuensis tabuensis (Gmelin, 1789)

1789   *Rallus tabuensis* Gmelin, Syst. Nat., **1**:717 (Tonga Tabu, Tahiti, and neighboring islands)
1789   *Rallus tahitiensis* Gmelin, Syst. Nat., **1**:717 (Tahiti and Friendly Islands)
1854   *Porzana vitiensis* Hartlaub, Journ. f. Orn., **2**:169 (based on *"Zapornia spilinota"* Peale, 1848; *not* Gould, 1841. Ovalau, Fiji)
1856   *Zapornia umbrina* Cassin, Proc. Acad. Nat. Sci. Phila., **8**:254 (Ovalau, Fiji)

Description: Head and underparts slate-black; wings, back, and rump very dark reddish brown; under tail-coverts black with white bars.
Soft Parts: Bill black; iris red; feet red (orange in young).
Measurements: Wing ♂ 81, ♀ 80; tail ♂ 41, ♀ 40; bill 19; tarsus 28.
Range: American Samoa (Manua Islands, Tau)
   Austral Islands (Rapa, Tubuai)
   Ducie
   Fiji (Kandavu, Ngau, Ono-I-Lau, Ovalau, Taveuni, Viti Levu)
   Marquesas Islands (Hatutu, Nuku Hiva)
   Niue
   Oeno
   Society Islands (Moorea, Raiatea, Tahiti)
   Tuamotu Archipelago (Apataki, Aratika, Hiti, Magareva, Manihi, Manui, Raraka, Tikehau, Toau)
   Western Samoa (Savaii)

Remarks: A shy rail of freshwater marshes and sometimes salt marshes, it is usually found at dawn and dusk.

WHITE-BROWED RAIL   PLATE 9

Poliolimnas cinereus tannensis (Forster, 1844)

1844 *Rallus tannensis* Forster, Descr. Anim., ed. Licht., p. 275 (Tanna Island, New Hebrides)

Description: Head and lores dark olive-gray; upper back dark olive-brown; wings, back, and tail dark brown, feathers with paler margins; patch above lores; stripe extending from bill under and behind eyes; chin and upper throat white; sides of throat and breast gray; flanks olive-gray; center of belly whitish; under tail-coverts pale rufous. Immature—browner and paler above; underparts white, washed with buff.
Soft Parts: Bill yellow-brown; iris red; feet greenish yellow.
Measurements: Wing ♂ 95, ♀ 92; tail ♂ 48, ♀ 47; bill 23; tarsus 38.
Range: American Samoa (Manua Islands, Tutuila)
   Fiji (Ngau, Ovalau, Viti Levu)
   Western Samoa (Savaii, Upolu)

Remarks: This is a shy bird of the marshes and rice fields and is not common.

PURPLE SWAMPHEN   PLATE 9

Porphyrio porphyrio samoensis Peale, 1848

1848   *Porphyrio samoensis* Peale, U. S. Expl. Expd., **8**:220 (Upolu, Samoa)

Description: Hind crown and neck brownish black; upper back dark blue; mantle, wings, and tail olive-brown; wing shoulders turquoise-blue with a black base to feathers; breast and belly dark purplish blue; under tail-coverts white.

Soft-Parts: Bill and shield red; iris red (brown in young birds); feet light red.

Measurements: Wing ♂ 212, ♀ 208; tail ♂ 75, ♀ 71; bill 38; tarsus 70.

Range: American Samoa (Aunuu, Manua Islands, Ofu, Olosega, Tau, Tutuila)
        Western Samoa (Savaii, Upolu)

Porphyrio porphyrio vitiensis Peale, 1848

1848   *Porphyrio vitiensis* Peale, U. S. Expl. Expd., **8**:221 (Ovalau, Fiji Islands)

Description: Differs from *P. p. samoensis* by having the upperparts greener brown and the underparts duller.

Range: Fiji (Kandavu, Matathawa Levu, Ono-I-Lau, Ovalau, Taveuni, Uea)
        Niue
        Rotuma
        Tonga (Ava, Fonualei, Late, Mango, Niuafoo, Nomuka, Oua, Tofonga, Tonumea)

Remarks: A bird of the swamps and lowland cultivated areas, it is often found in taro fields, where it feeds on newly sprouted grass shoots.

SAMOAN WOOD RAIL   PLATE 9

Pareudiastes pacificus Hartlaub and Finsch, 1871

1871   *Pareudiastes pacificus* Hartlaub and Finsch, Proc. Zool. Soc. London, p. 25 (Savaii, Samoan Islands)

Description: Entire bird blackish; upperparts somewhat olivaceous; breast bluish gray.

Soft Parts: Bill light red, frontal shield yellow; iris red-brown; feet red.

Measurements: Three unsexed specimens = wing 125; tail 36; bill 30; tarsus 39.
Range: Western Samoa (Savaii)

Remarks: The habits of this bird are unrecorded. It has not been seen since 1873 and is possibly extinct. It was probably flightless.

CHARADRIIDAE   PLOVERS

PACIFIC GOLDEN PLOVER   PLATE 12

Pluvialis dominica fulva (Gmelin, 1789)

1789   *Charadrius fulvus* Gmelin, Syst. Nat., **1**:687 (Tahiti)

Description: Nonbreeding plumage—top of head, back, rump, tail, and scapulars black with buffy gold margins; primaries black; sides of head and faint eye stripe golden with fine brown streaks; chin buffy white; throat, breast, and flanks gray with brown shaft streaks and margins to feathers; belly and under tail-coverts white. Breeding plumage—upperparts golden; underparts black.
Soft Parts: Bill blackish brown; iris dark brown; feet black.
Measurements: Wing ♂ 164, ♀ 162; tail ♂ 60, ♀ 58; bill 23; tarsus 41.
Range: American Samoa (Manua Islands, Olosega, Rose Island, Tutuila)
Austral Islands (Rurutu)
Fiji (Lakemba, Leleuvia, Moala, Ngasele Bay, Nukulau, Taveuni, Thithia, Viti Levu, Welangilala)
Marquesas Islands (Nuku Hiva)
Niue
Society Islands (Bora-Bora, Maiao, Moorea, Mopelia, Raiatea, Scilly, Tahiti, Tetiaroa)
Tonga (Niuatoputapu, Putuputua, Tokulu)
Tuamotu Archipelago (Ahe, Apataki, Fakarava, Hao, Hiti, Katiu, Kaukura, Makatea, Makemo, Marutea, Matahiva, Rangiroa, Raraka, Raroia, Tahanea, Taiaro, Takapoto, Tenaruga, Tepoto, Tikehau, Tikei, ?Toau, Tuanake, Vanavana)
Wallis
Western Samoa (Apolima, Savaii, Upolu)

Remarks: This is a common wintering bird from the north and may be found most anywhere along the coast.

MONGOLIAN PLOVER PLATE 12

Charadrius mongolus mongolus Pallas, 1776

1776 *Charadrius mongolus* Pallas, Reise Versch. Prov. Russ. Reichs, **3**:700 (salt lakes toward the Mongolian border = Kulussutai, probably on the Onon River, Siberia)

Description: Nonbreeding plumage—upperparts pale brown; primaries black; forehead and eye stripe whitish; sides of head olive-gray; chin and throat white; breast band olive-gray; belly and under tail-coverts white.
Soft Parts: Bill black; iris dark brown; feet black.
Measurements: Wing ♂ 136, ♀ 131; tail ♂ 54, ♀ 52; bill 18; tarsus 27.
Range: Fiji (Viti Levu)

Remarks: A rare winter visitor to Fiji from Asia, this bird has been recorded only a few times.

BANDED DOTTEREL PLATE 12

Charadrius bicinctus Jardine and Selby, 1827

1827 *Charadrius bicinctus* Jardine and Selby, Ill. Orn., **1**, pl. 28 (New Holland = New South Wales)

Description: Forehead and line over eye white; a black line between forehead and crown and also from the bill to the eye; upperparts olive-brown; underparts white, except for a black band on the lower throat and a dark chestnut band on the breast. Wintering birds much duller.
Soft Parts: Bill black; iris blackish brown, eyelids red; feet yellowish white.
Measurements: Wing ♂ 131, ♀ 128; tail ♂ 55, ♀ 54; bill 20; tarsus 28.
Range: Fiji (Ono-I-Lau, Viti Levu)

Remarks: This bird is a rare visitor to Fiji (once).

PLATE 10

A   PARASITIC JAEGER
      (*Stercorarius parasiticus*), male—page 59

B   POMARINE JAEGER
      (*Stercorarius pomarinus*), male—page 58

C   WHIMBREL
      (*Numenius phaeopus*), male—page 52

D   EASTERN CURLEW
      (*Numenius madagascariensis*), male—page 53

E   BRISTLE-THIGHED CURLEW
      (*Numenius tahitiensis*), male—page 52

F   BAR-TAILED GODWIT
      (*Limosa lapponica*), male—page 53

PLATE 10

SANDSTRÖM

PLATE 11

PLATE 11

SANDSTRÖM

PLATE 12

A   PACIFIC GOLDEN PLOVER
    (*Pluvialis dominica*), male—page 44

B   MONGOLIAN PLOVER
    (*Charadrius mongolus*), male—page 45

C   BANDED DOTTEREL
    (*Charadrius bicinctus*), male—page 45

D   COMMON TERN
    (*Sterna hirundo*), male—page 60

E   ROSEATE TERN
    (*Sterna dougallii*), male—page 60

F   BLACK-NAPED TERN
    (*Sterna sumatrana*), male—page 61

G   BLUE-GRAY NODDY
    (*Procelsterna cerulea*), male—page 64

H   WHITE TERN
    (*Gygis alba*), male—page 65

PLATE 12

SANDSTRÖM

WHIMBREL   PLATE 10

Numenius phaeopus variegatus (Scopoli, 1786)

1786   *Tantalus variegatus* Scopoli, Del. Flor. et Faun. Insubr., p. 92 (Luzon)

Description: Top of head dark brown with a gray stripe down the center; upperparts gray-brown mottled with gray; rump whitish; tail dark brown with light brown bars; superciliary gray-buff; sides of face and throat gray, finely streaked with brown; breast buff, heavily streaked with brown; center of belly whitish; flanks, thighs, and under tail-coverts dirty white with brown bars.

Soft Parts: Bill black, base of lower mandible dark brown; iris dark brown; feet plumbeous.

Measurements: Wing ♂ 238, ♀ 230; tail ♂ 116, ♀ 112; bill 90; tarsus 50.

Range: Fiji (Nukulau, Taveuni, Viti Levu)
         The Samoas (once)

Remarks: This rare straggler has been recorded from Fiji and once from Samoa in 1911; the latter specimen may be *N. p. hudsonicus* from North America, which lacks the whitish rump patch. Other Whimbrels have been seen in Fiji, but positive subspecific identification is unknown.

BRISTLE-THIGHED CURLEW   PLATE 10

Numenius tahitiensis (Gmelin, 1789)

1789   *Scolopax tahitiensis* Gmelin, Syst. Nat., **1**:656 (Tahiti, Society Islands)

Description: Upperparts brown mottled with buffy white; rump buffy white; tail rufous with dark brown bars; chin white; throat, breast, and flanks white with dark brown shaft streaks to feathers; rest of underparts white with a pale rufous wash.

Soft Parts: Bill black; iris brown; feet slate.

Measurements: Wing ♂ 242, ♀ 235; tail ♂ 97, ♀ 95; bill 95; tarsus 53.

Range: American Samoa (Rose Island, Tutuila)
         Ducie
         Fiji (Nggele Levu)
         Henderson Island
         Marquesas Islands (Eiao, Fatu Huku, Hatutu, Nuku Hiva)
         Niue

Oeno
Pitcairn Island
Society Islands (Maiao, Mopelia, Scilly, Tahiti, Tetiaroa)
Tonga (Putuputua, Toku)
Tuamotu Archipelago (Ahunui, Apataki, Hiti, Kauehi, Make-
    mo, Maria, Marutea, Matahiva, Maturei-Vavao, Paraoa, Ran-
    giroa, Tahanea, Tenarare, Tenaruga, Tikehau, Toau,
    Tuanake, Tureia, Vanavana)
Western Samoa (Apolima, Savaii, Upolu)

Remarks: This is one of the most common shore birds in the South
Pacific.

EASTERN CURLEW   PLATE 10

Numenius madagascariensis (Linnaeus, 1766)

1766   *Scolopax madagascariensis* Linnaeus, Syst. Nat., **1**:242 ("Madagascar";
    error = Macassar, Celebes)

Description: Upperparts gray-brown heavily streaked with dark brown;
chin pale buff with fine brown shaft streaks; sides of face and rest of
underparts buffy streaked with brown.
Soft Parts: Bill black, base of lower mandible flesh color; iris brown; feet
dark gray.
Measurements: Wing ♂ 320, ♀ 314; tail ♂ 146, ♀ 130; bill 195; tarsus
95.
Range: Fiji (Rewa estuary, Viti Levu)
      Western Samoa (Savaii)

Remarks: This curlew strays into the South Pacific from farther west.

BAR-TAILED GODWIT   PLATE 10

Limosa lapponica baueri Naumann, 1836

1836   *Limosa Baueri* Naumann, Handb. Natürg. Vög. Deutsch., **8**:429 (Victoria,
    Australia)

Description: Upperparts gray-brown mottled with dark brown; rump
gray-white barred with dark brown; tail dark brown with light bars; face,

chin, and throat buff with fine brown streaks; rest of underparts pure whitish.

Soft Parts: Bill, terminal half blackish, basal half pinkish; iris brown; feet dark brown.

Measurements: Wing ♂ 239, ♀ 231; tail ♂ 82, ♀ 80; bill 108; tarsus 57.

Range: American Samoa (Rose Island, Tutuila)
Fiji (Nukulau, Ono-I-Lau, Rewa estuary, Tomberua, Viti Levu)
Western Samoa (Upolu)

Remarks: This bird is a winter visitor from the south and is not common.

WANDERING TATTLER   PLATE 11

Tringa incana incana (Gmelin, 1789)

1789 *Scolopax incana* Gmelin, Syst. Nat., **1**:658 (Eimeo = Moorea, Society Islands)

Description: Upperparts gray; eye stripe whitish; underparts dull whitish with a slight grayish breast band in wintering birds; summer birds have underparts barred.

Soft Parts: Bill black, base of lower mandible gray-brown; iris dark brown; feet yellowish.

Measurements: Wing ♂ 163, ♀ 157; tail ♂ 69, ♀ 67; bill 40; tarsus 30.

Range: American Samoa (Manua Islands, Olosega, Rose Island, Tutuila)
Austral Islands (Papa, Raevavae, Rimatara, Rurutu, Tubuai)
Ducie
Fiji (Kandavu, Lakemba, Leleuvia, Nukulau, Rewa estuary, Taveuni, Viti Levu, Wakaya, Yalewa Kalou)
Henderson Island
Marquesas Islands (Dapu, Eiao, Hiva Oa, Motuiti, Nuku Hiva)
Niue
Society Islands (Bora-Bora, Huamiua, Maiao, Moorea, Raiatea, Scilly, Tahiti, Tetiaroa)
Tonga (Fonoifua, Niuafoo, Niuatoputapu, Oua)
Tuamotu Archipelago (Ahe, Ahunui, Anaa, Aratika, Aukena, Faaite, Fakahina, Fakapoio, Fakarava, Hao, Kamaka, Kauehi, Magareva, Makatea, Makemo, Manihi, Maria, Marutea, Matahiva, Maturei-Vavao, Motu Teiko, Napuka, Nihiru, Rangiroa, Raroia, Tahanea, Takapoto, Takaroa, Temoe, Tenararo, Tenaruga, Tikei, Toau, Tuanake, Tureia)
Western Samoa (Savaii, Upolu)

Tringa incana brevipes (Vieillot, 1816)

1816   *Totanus brevipes* Vieillot, Nouv. Dict. d'Hist. Nat., **6**:410 (no locality = Timor)

Description: Differs from *T. i. incana* by having the upperparts paler gray and the eye stripe and underparts purer white.
Range: Fiji (Viti Levu)

Remarks: This is one of the most common of the shore birds.

TEREK SANDPIPER   PLATE 11

Xenus cinereus (Güldenstaedt, 1774)

1774   *Scolopax cinerea* Güldenstaedt, Novi Comm. Sci. Petropol., **19**:473 (Caspian Sea)

Description: Upperparts olive-gray, feathers with dark shaft streaks becoming blackish on the back; superciliary pale gray; chin white; throat white finely streaked with brownish gray; rest of underparts white.
Soft Parts: Bill black, lower mandible base yellowish; iris dark brown; feet olive-gray.
Measurements: Wing ♂ 130, ♀ 125; tail ♂ 60, ♀ 56; bill 50; tarsus 26.
Range: Fiji (Viti Levu)

Remarks: This sandpiper is a rare visitor to the South Pacific.

TURNSTONE   PLATE 11

Arenaria interpes interpes (Linnaeus, 1758)

1758   *Tringa interpes* Linnaeus, Syst. Nat., **1**:148 (Gotland, Sweden)
1826   *Tringa oahuensis* Bloxham, in Byron's Voy. "Blonde," p. 251 (Oahu, Hawaiian Islands)

Description: Winter plumage—upperparts and breast band mottled gray-brown; prominent wing stripe white; chin, upper throat, belly, and under tail-coverts white. Breeding plumage—more colorful, face black and white; majority of upperparts dull chestnut.
Soft Parts: Bill black; iris brown; feet orange-red.
Measurements: Wing ♂ 150, ♀ 146; tail ♂ 56, ♀ 54; bill 24; tarsus 24.

Range: American Samoa (Manua Islands, Olosega, Rose Island, Tutuila)
Fiji (Leleuvia, Nggele Levu, Nukulau, Ono-I-Lau, Welangilala, Yasawa)
Tonga (Tokulu)
Western Samoa (Apolima, Savaii, Upolu)

Remarks: This is a common visitor to the South Pacific from the north.

TUAMOTU SANDPIPER   PLATE 11

Prosobonia cancellata (Gmelin, 1789)

1789   *Tringa cancellata* Gmelin, Syst. Nat., **1**:675 (in insula Nativitatis Christi = Christmas Island, Pacific Ocean)
1848   *Tringa parvirostris* Peale, U. S. Expl. Expd., **8**:235 (Dog or Honden Island, Tuamotu)

Description: Pale phase—upperparts brown streaked and mottled with white; eye stripe white; chin whitish; throat, breast, and flanks barred brown and white; central belly white. Dark phase—darker brown with the white of the eye stripe, chin, and belly much reduced. Many intermediate individuals exist and both color phases interbreed.
Soft Parts: Bill black; iris brown; feet black.
Measurements: Wing ♂ 103, ♀ 103; tail ♂ 58, ♀ 55; bill 16; tarsus 24.
Range: Line Islands (Christmas Atoll) (one record)
Tuamotu Archipelago (Fakarava, Hiti, Kamaka, Katiu, Kauehi, Makaroa, Manui, Maria, Marutea, Maturei-Vavao, Pinaki, Pukapuka, Rangiroa, Raraka, Tahanea, Tenararo, Tenaruga, Tepoto, Tuanake, Vahaga, Vanavana)

Remarks: This sandpiper lives on uninhabited islands and occasionally will visit inhabited ones. It is usually found feeding in broken coral rubble.

TAHITIAN SANDPIPER   PLATE 11

Prosobonia leucoptera (Gmelin, 1789)

1789   *Tringa leucoptera* Gmelin, Syst. Nat., **1**:678 (Tahiti and Eimeo Islands)
1906   *Prosobonia ellisi* Sharpe, Bull. Brit. Orn. Cl., **16**:86 (Eimeo Island)

Description: Top of head and mantle blackish brown; lower back and rump ferruginous; tail rufous, the two central rectrices black; chin, upper throat, and a spot behind the eye whitish; rest of underparts ferruginous.
Soft Parts: Unrecorded.
Measurements: Wing 113; tail 54; bill 24; tarsus 34.
Range: Society Islands (Moorea, Tahiti) (extinct)

Remarks: Only the unique type exists, which was collected by the Cook Expedition (1773). Two other specimens may have been collected, but their whereabouts is unknown. This species has not been seen since it was first discovered.

SANDERLING   PLATE 11

Calidris alba (Pallas, 1764)

1764   *Trynga alba* Pallas, in Vroeg's Cat., p. 7 (North Sea)

Description: Wintering birds—upperparts grayish white, streaked and mottled with browns and blacks; wing with a broad white stripe; underparts white. Breeding plumage—upperparts and breast rusty.
Soft Parts: Bill black; iris brown; feet black.
Measurements: Wing ♂ 126, ♀ 123; tail ♂ 44, ♀ 43; bill 26; tarsus 23.
Range: Ducie
Fiji (Ono, Ono-I-Lau, Tomberua, Viti Levu)

Remarks: The sanderling is probably a common visitor to the South Pacific, but it has been recorded from only a few localities.

LITTLE STINT   PLATE 11

Calidris ruficollis (Pallas, 1776)

1776   *Trynga ruficollis* Pallas, Reise Versch. Prov. Russ. Reichs, 3:700 ("Circa lacus salsos Dauriae campestris" = Kulussutai, southern Transbaikalia)

Description: Upperparts gray-brown, some feathers having dark shaft streaks; rump, tail, and primaries dark brown; underparts white with a gray band across the chest.

Soft Parts: Bill black; iris brown; feet black.
Measurements: Wing ♂ 96, ♀ 94; tail ♂ 43, ♀ 42; bill 18; tarsus 20.
Range: Fiji (Viti Levu) (twice)

Remarks: A rare sandpiper in the South Pacific.

SHARP-TAILED SANDPIPER   PLATE 11

Calidris acuminata (Horsfield, 1821)

1821   *Totanus acuminatus* Horsfield, Trans. Linn. Soc. London, **13**:192 (Java)

Description: Crown dull rufous streaked with black; upperparts brown
streaked with dark brown feathers having buffy edges; underparts gray-
white; feathers of lower throat and breast have dark brown shaft streaks.
Soft Parts: Bill black, base of lower mandible brown; iris dark brown;
feet olive-yellow.
Measurements: Wing ♂ 128, ♀ 124; tail ♂ 55, ♀ 53; bill 26; tarsus 28.
Range: Fiji (Viti Levu) (twice)

Remarks: A rare visitor to the South Pacific.

STERCORARIIDAE   SKUAS

POMARINE JAEGER   PLATE 10

Stercorarius pomarinus (Temminck, 1815)

1815   *Lestris pomarinus* Temminck, Man. d' Orn., p. 514 (Arctic regions of
       Europe)

Description: Forehead and crown dark brownish black; collar white;
rest of upperparts dark brown; chin and throat white; breast white with
a few brown bars; upper belly white; lower belly, thighs, and under tail-
coverts brown.
Soft Parts: Bill dark brown; iris brown; feet blackish brown.
Measurements: Wing ♂ 360, ♀ 353; tail ♂ 240, ♀ 232; bill 40; tarsus 47.
Range: Visits the Society Islands (Tahiti).

Remarks: This rare visitor to the South Pacific from the Northern
Hemisphere should be looked for on other island groups.

PARASITIC JAEGER   PLATE 10

Stercorarius parasiticus (Linnaeus, 1758)

1758   *Larus parasiticus* Linnaeus, Syst. Nat., **1**:136 (Sweden)

Description: Upperparts dark brown; underparts white or brownish.
Soft Parts: Bill horn color; iris brown; feet black.
Measurements: Wing ♂ 349, ♀ 340; tail ♂ 208, ♀ 197; bill 34; tarsus 42.
Range: Visits the Society Islands (Tahiti).

Remarks: This rare visitor to the South Pacific from the Northern Hemisphere may appear on other islands.

LARIDAE   GULLS AND TERNS

SILVER GULL   PLATE 13

Larus novaehollandiae Stephens, 1826

1826   *Larus Novae-Hollandiae* Stephens, in Shaw's Gen. Zool., **13**:196 (New South Wales)

Description: A pure white gull with a gray mantle; primaries mostly black wth white spots. Immature—mottled brown and gray above; tail with dark band.
Soft Parts: Bill red; iris white; feet red. Immature—bill, iris, and feet brownish.
Measurements: Wing ♂ 275, ♀ 268; tail ♂ 114, ♀ 110; bill 33; tarsus 43.
Range: Visits the ?Marquesas Islands and the ?Society Islands. Within the area covered by this book, this species is known from only a few 19th century sight records. No specimens are known; the subspecies is therefore indeterminate.

FRANKLIN'S GULL   PLATE 13

Larus pipixcan Wagler, 1831

1831   *Larus Pipixcan* Wagler, Isis, col. 515 (Mexico)

Description: Head black, but white in wintering birds; mantle gray; primaries black with terminal white spots; rump, tail, and underparts white.
Soft Parts: Bill maroon; iris brown; feet dull red.

Measurements: Wing ♂ 285, ♀ 278; tail 100; bill 32; tarsus 40.
Range: Visits the Marquesas Islands (two records) from the eastern Pacific.

COMMON TERN   PLATE 12
Sterna hirundo Linnaeus, 1758
1758   *Sterna Hirundo* Linnaeus, Syst. Nat., **1**:137 (Europe, restricted to Sweden)

Description: Top of head and nape black in breeding birds; forehead and front of crown white in wintering birds; mantle gray; rump and forked tail white; all of underparts white. Immature—like winter adult, but back more or less faintly barred with brown and black; tail grayish, with fork shorter; a blackish patch on shoulder.
Soft Parts: Bill blackish with varying amount of red at base; iris dark brown; feet dull red.
Measurements: Wing ♂ 240, ♀ 234; tail 130; bill 40; tarsus 21.
Range: Visits Fiji. Subspecies is uncertain.

ROSEATE TERN   PLATE 12
Sterna dougallii bangsi Mathews, 1912
1912   *Sterna dougallii bangsi* Mathews, Bds. Austr., **2**:364 (Foochow, China)

Description: Top of head and nape black; upperparts very pale gray; outer three primaries dark gray-black; underparts white. Winter plumage—forehead white.
Soft Parts: Bill black with varying amount of red at base; iris dark brown; feet coral-red. Immature—like Common Tern immature, but forehead with less white; rump and tail much paler than mantle.
Measurements: Wing ♂ 225, ♀ 218; tail 140; bill 40; tarsus 18.
Range: Visits Tonga and the Tuamotu Archipelago from Asia.

SOOTY TERN   PLATE 13
Sterna fuscata serrata Wagler, 1830
1830   *Sterna serrata* Wagler, Natursyst. Amphib., p. 89 (New Caledonia)

Description: Forehead white; stripe from bill to eyes black; rest of upperparts black; underparts white. Immature—blackish above, with white tips to mantle feathers; underparts brown.
Soft Parts: Bill black; iris blackish; feet black.
Measurements: Wing ♂ 305, ♀ 290; tail 212; bill 41; tarsus 23.
Range: Breeds on the Austral Islands, the Cook Islands, Fiji, the Marquesas Islands, the Samoas, the Society Islands, Tonga, and the Tuamotu Archipelago.

Remarks: This species is in need of revision: *serrata* is used by Mayr and Mathews in later publications, but *oahuensis* has been suggested by Peters.

BRIDLED TERN   PLATE 13

Sterna anaethetus anaethetus Scopoli, 1786

1786   *Sterna Anaethetus* Scopoli, Del. Flor. et Faun. Insubr., p. 92 (in Guinea = Panay, Philippines)

Description: Forehead and stripe over eyes white; crown and lores black; nape white; rest of upperparts brownish gray; all underparts white. Immature—cap paler; back heavily barred.
Soft Parts: Bill black; iris dark brown; feet dark gray.
Measurements: Wing ♂ 270, ♀ 262; tail 180; bill 41; tarsus 19.
Range: Visits Fiji, the Samoas, and Tonga from the western Pacific.

GRAY-BACKED TERN   PLATE 13

Sterna lunata Peale, 1848

1848   *Sterna lunata* Peale, U. S. Expl. Expd., **8**:277 (Vincennes Island, Paumotu Group)

Description: Forehead and eye stripe white; crown, nape, and lores black; mantle, rump, and tail gray; outer tail feathers with outer margins white; underparts white.
Soft Parts: Bill black; iris brown; feet black.
Measurements: Wing ♂ 270, ♀ 264; tail 175; bill 46; tarsus 19.
Range: Breeds on Fiji, the Society Islands, and the Tuamotu Archipelago. Visits the Marquesas Islands, the Samoas, and Tonga.

BLACK-NAPED TERN   PLATE 12

Sterna sumatrana sumatrana Raffles, 1822

1822   *Sterna Sumatrana* Raffles, Trans. Linn. Soc. London, **13**:329 (Sumatra)

Description: Top of head white; black line runs through eyes and joins on the nape; upperparts pale gray; outer primary edged with black; underparts white. Immature—mottled gray-brown on nape and mantle; bill and legs yellowish.
Soft Parts: Bill black; iris dark brown; feet black.
Measurements: Wing ♂ 230, ♀ 225; tail 150; bill 43; tarsus 18.
Range: Breeds on Fiji. Visits the Samoas and Tonga.

PLATE 13

A

B

C

D

E

F

G

H

PLATE 13

SANDSTRÖM

CRESTED TERN   PLATE 13

Sterna bergi cristatus Stephens, 1826

1826   *Sterna cristata* Stephens, in Shaw's Gen. Zool., **13**:146 (China)

Description: Forehead white; crown and crest black; hind neck white; rest of upperparts gray; underparts white. Nonbreeding—crown mottled with white. Immature—like nonbreeding adult but mantle mottled brownish.

Soft Parts: Bill greenish yellow; iris black; feet black.

Measurements: Wing ♂ 330, ♀ 324; tail 155; bill 58; tarsus 28.

Range: Breeds on Fiji, the Society Islands, Tonga, and the Tuamotu Archipelago. Visits the Samoas.

BLUE-GRAY NODDY   PLATE 12

Procelsterna cerulea (F. D. Bennett, 1840)

1840   *Sterna Cerulea* F. D. Bennett, Narr. Whaling Voy., **2**:248 (Christmas Island, Pacific Ocean)

Description: Entire bird blue-gray; in the pale phase the underparts are lighter; both phases have a broken white eye-ring.

Soft Parts: Bill black; iris brown; feet black with yellow webs.

Measurements: Wing ♂ 190, ♀ 184; tail 103; bill 27; tarsus 23.

Range: Breeds on Fiji, Henderson Island, the Marquesas Islands, Pitcairn Island, the Samoas, the Society Islands, Tonga, and the Tuamotu Archipelago. Visits Ducie.

Remarks: This species is in need of revision as many subspecies have been described and their status is uncertain.

BROWN NODDY   PLATE 13

Anous stolidus pileatus (Scopoli, 1786)

1786   *Sterna pileata* Scopoli, Del. Flor. et Faun. Insubr., p. 92 (no locality = Philippines)

Description: Forehead and part of crown whitish; rest of bird brownish gray. Immature—lacks light cap.

Soft Parts: Bill black; iris brown; feet red-brown.

Measurements: Wing ♂ 260, ♀ 252; tail 148; bill 47; tarsus 21.

Range: Breeds on the Austral Islands, the Cook Islands, Ducie, Fiji, Henderson Island, the Marquesas Islands, Oeno, Pitcairn Island, the Samoas, the Society Islands, Tonga, and the Tuamotu Archipelago.

BLACK NODDY   PLATE 13

Anous tenuirostris minutus Boie, 1844

1844   *Anous minutus* Boie, Isis, col. 188 (New Holland = Raine Island, Australia)

Description: Top of head pale grayish white, rest of bird sooty black. A paler phase also exists that is more gray overall.
Soft Parts: Bill black; iris blackish; feet black.
Measurements: Wing ♂ 226, ♀ 222; tail 115; bill 50; tarsus 19.
Range: Breeds on Fiji, the Marquesas Islands, the Samoas, the Society Islands, Tonga, and the Tuamotu Archipelago. Visits the Austral Islands.

WHITE TERN   PLATE 12

Gygis alba candida (Gmelin, 1789)

1789   *Sterna candida* Gmelin, Syst. Nat., **1**:609 (Christmas Islands, Pacific Ocean)

Description: Entire bird pure white; shafts of primaries and rectrices blackish. Immature—a black spot behind the eye; mantle with brownish spots.
Soft Parts: Bill black, bluish at base; iris black; feet blue-black.
Measurements: Wing ♂ 245, ♀ 242; tail ♂ 115, ♀ 112; bill 46; tarsus 10.
Range: Breeds on the Austral Islands, the Cook Islands, Danger Atoll, Ducie, Fiji, Henderson Island, Oeno, Pitcairn Island, the Samoas, the Society Islands, Tonga, and the Tuamotu Archipelago.

Gygis alba microrhyncha Saunders, 1876

1876   *Gygis microrhyncha* Saunders, Proc. Zool. Soc. London, p. 668 (Marquesas Islands)

Description: Differs from *G. a. candida* by having the shaft streaks of the wings and tail much paler, almost white. The bill is more slender and shorter (40) and the blue extends farther toward the tip.
Range: Breeds on the Marquesas Islands.

Remarks: This beautiful tern is common around most all the islands. The subspecific affiliations of many of the island groups still have to be worked out.

ROCK DOVE   PLATE 17

Columba livia Gmelin, 1789

1789   *Columba livia* Gmelin, Syst. Nat., **1**:769 (no type locality = southern Europe)

Description: In the wild state this common city pigeon is usually dark gray with bluish bars on the wings. However, through breeding and domestication it now appears in a wide variety of colors.

Soft Parts: Bill gray; iris dark red; feet maroon.

Measurements: Wing ♂ 240, ♀ 235; tail ♂ 115, ♀ 112; bill 23; tarsus 30.

Range: Fiji (Viti Levu)
   Marquesas Islands (Ua Huka)
   Society Islands (Bora-Bora, Moorea, Raiatea, Tahiti)
   Tuamotu Archipelago (Makatea)
   Western Samoa (Savaii, Upolu)

Remarks: This pigeon has been introduced throughout the world and has been officially recorded from only a few islands in the South Pacific. However, as it spreads with modern civilization, it is to be expected that it will be found on most any of the islands.

WHITE-THROATED PIGEON   PLATE 17

Columba vitiensis vitiensis Quoy and Gaimard, 1830

1830   *Columba vitiensis* Quoy and Gaimard, Voy. "Astrolabe," Zool., **1**:246 (Fiji Islands)

Description: Male—top of head, back, and rump dark gray heavily washed with glossy green; wings and tail dark brownish black; chin, throat, and cheeks whitish; breast vinaceous gray; belly bright vinaceous. Female—similar to male but much duller above.

Soft Parts: Bill purplish red; iris red; feet reddish black.

Measurements: Wing ♂ 226, ♀ 217; tail ♂ 160, ♀ 155; bill 26; tarsus 26.

Range: Fiji (Aiwa, Avea, Fulanga, Kambara, Kandavu, Katafanga, Kimbombo, Kio, Koro, Makongai, Mango, Marambo, Matathawa Levu, Mbatiki, Moala, Mothe, Munia, Nairai, Naitaumba, Na-

67

menalala, Namuka-I-Lau, Nathula, Ngau, Nggalito, Ongea Levu, Ono, Ovalau, Taveuni, Thikombia Ilau, Thithia, Totoya, Tuvutha, Vanua Kula, Vanua Levu, Vanuambalavu, Vanuavatu, Vatulele, Vatuvara, Viti Levu, Wakaya, Waya, Yanutha, Yasawa, Yathata, Yaukuve Levu)

Columba vitiensis castaneiceps Peale, 1848

1848 *Columba castaneiceps* Peale, U. S. Expl. Expd., **8**:187 (Upolu, Samoa)

Description: Differs from *C. v. vitiensis* by having the top of the head purplish, upperparts more heavily washed with glossy green, cheeks and throat whiter, and underparts slate-gray.

Range: Western Samoa (Apolima, Manono, Savaii, Upolu)

Remarks: A very common and unwary pigeon from the seacoast to the mountain tops, this bird usually sits on palm fronds and limbs near fruit. In flight it usually looks black.

SPOTTED DOVE   PLATE 14

Streptopelia chinensis tigrina (Temminck, 1810)

1810 *Columba Tigrina* Temminck, in Knip's Les Pigeons, p. 94 (Timor and Batavia = Java)

Description: Forehead light gray; top of head and neck pinkish gray; nuchal collar black with white spots; upperparts brown; feathers of wing-coverts have dark shaft streaks; outer tail feathers with white tips; chin light gray; throat and breast vinaceous red; belly and under tail-coverts buffy.

Soft Parts: Bill black; iris gray; feet pink.

Measurements: Wing 145; tail 138; bill 16; tarsus 24.

Range: Introduced from southeast Asia to Fiji (Nukulau, Taveuni, Viti Levu).

Remarks: Usually found in and around towns, this dove feeds on the ground and is rather tame.

68

PLATE 14

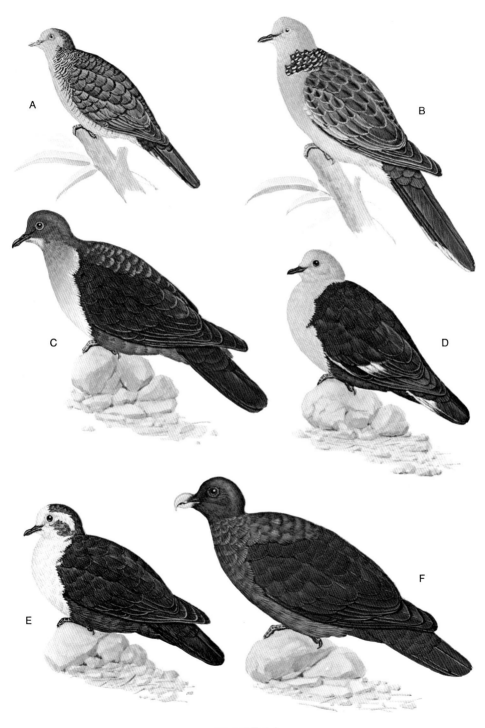

PLATE 14

SANDSTRÖM

ZEBRA DOVE PLATE 14

Geopelia striata ssp. (Linnaeus, 1766)

1766 *Columba striata* Linnaeus, Syst. Nat., **1**:242 (East Indies = Java)

Description: Forehead gray; head brown; back, rump, and wings brown with black bars; tail brown, outer feathers with white tips; throat pure blue-gray; sides of throat, breast, and belly buffy white with fine black bars; center of breast vinaceous red; belly and under tail-coverts whitish.

Soft Parts: Bill bluish; iris pale blue; feet red.

Measurements: Wing 98; tail 102; bill 12; tarsus 16.

Range: Introduced to the Society Islands (Tahiti).

Remarks: This dove is often seen feeding on the ground along roadways and in the suburbs of well-populated areas.

SOCIETY ISLANDS GROUND DOVE PLATE 14

Gallicolumba erythroptera (Gmelin, 1789)

1789 *Columba erythroptera* Gmelin, Syst. Nat., **1**:775 (Moorea, Society Islands)

1789 *Columba eimeensis* Gmelin, Syst. Nat., **1**:784 (Eimeo)

1829 *Columba leucophrys* Wagler, Isis, **7**, col. 743 (Otaheitee)

1848 *Peristera pectoralis* Peale, U. S. Expl. Expd., **8**:205 (Aratika, Tuamotu Group)

1892 *Phlogoenas albicollis* Salvadori, Bull. Brit. Orn. Cl., **1**:10 (Bow Island, Tuamotu Group)

Description: Male—forehead and stripe over eye white; top of head and ear-coverts dark gray; upperparts dark brown; upperback and wing-coverts washed with dark purplish red; chin, throat, and breast white; breast, belly, and under tail-coverts brownish black. Female—upperparts dark reddish brown; mantle feathers tipped with gray; underparts reddish brown, breast paler; under tail-coverts blackish brown.

Soft Parts: Bill black; iris brown; feet black.

Measurements: Wing ♂ 149, ♀ 142; tail 82; bill 20; tarsus 33.

Range: Society Islands (Moorea, Tahiti)
Tuamotu Archipelago (Aratika, Maria, Tenararo, Tenaruga, Vanavana)

Remarks: A shy bird of the dense original forest, it is more often heard than seen. Its call is a low, hoarse moan.

FRIENDLY QUAIL DOVE PLATE 14

Gallicolumba stairi stairi (G. R. Gray, 1856)

1856   *Caloenas (Phlegoenas) Stairi* G. R. Gray, Proc. Zool. Soc. London, p. 115 (Samoa; error = Tonga)

1872   *Phl.[egoenas] vitiensis* Finsch, Journ. f. Orn., **20**:50 (Viti, Fiji)

Description: Male—forehead vinaceous; crown and hind neck gray washed with green; back and rump brown; wings brown; wing-coverts glossy purple; tail brown; chin and throat vinaceous, becoming paler on breast; belly and under tail-coverts brown. Female—differs from male by having upper and lower parts duller and more uniform in color. Immature—similar to female.

Soft Parts: Bill black; iris brown; feet dark red.

Measurements: Wing ♂ 151, ♀ 140; tail ♂ 88, ♀ 75; bill ♂ 19; tarsus ♂ 27.

Range: Western Samoa (Savaii, Upolu)

Gallicolumba stairi samoensis (Finsch, 1872)

1872   *Phl.[egoenas] samoensis* Finsch, Journ. f. Orn., **20**:50 (Samoa)

Description: Differs from *G. s. stairi* as follows: Male—gray patch on top of head is more extensive; upperparts more heavily washed with purplish; breast shield paler, with an almost white posterior border separating it from the belly. Female—browner. This race is also smaller.

Measurements: Wing ♂ 163, ♀ 151; tail ♂ 105, ♀ 98.

Range: Fiji (Aiwa, Kio, Koro, Makongai, Mbengga, Olorua, Ovalau, Rambi, Taveuni, Tuvutha, Vanuambalavu, Vatuvara, Viti Levu, Wakaya)

Tonga (Hunga Haapai, Hunga Tonga, Late, Nomuka Iki)

Remarks: This shy forest bird is usually found in virgin forest above 3500 feet in the Samoan Group. The Tongan birds are found at lower elevations and are much tamer.

MARQUESAS GROUND DOVE PLATE 14

Gallicolumba rubescens (Vieillot, 1818)

1818   *Columba rubescens* Vieillot, Nouv. Dict. d'Hist. Nat., p. 346 (Mankakiwa, Marquesas Islands)

Description: Male—head, neck, chin, throat, and breast gray; back and wing-coverts dark purplish red; rump and upper tail-coverts dark brown; wing primaries and secondaries brownish black with a white patch in the center of the feathers; tail white, with the terminal third dark brownish black and the central rectrices with less white, giving the entire tail a dark appearance; belly and under tail-coverts dark brownish black. Female—differs from the male by being generally darker.

Soft Parts: Bill black; iris brown; feet reddish black.

Measurements: Wing ♂ 128, ♀ 120; tail ♂ 79, ♀ 75; bill 17; tarsus 26.

Range: Marquesas Islands (Fatu Huku, Hatutu)

Remarks: Little is known of the habits of this bird; however, it probably lives on the ground in dense forest like other members of this group.

TOOTH-BILLED PIGEON   PLATE 14

Didunculus strigirostris (Jardine, 1845)

1845   *Gnathodon strigirostris* Jardine, Ann. Mag. Nat. Hist., **16**:9 (Australia; error = Samoa)

Description: Male—head, neck, and mantle glossy blackish green; back, rump, tail, and wing-coverts dark reddish chestnut; primaries and secondaries dark brown; underparts dull blackish with some of the feathers having silvery tips, especially on the breast; under tail-coverts dark chestnut. Female—similar to male but duller. Immature—upper and lower parts barred chestnut and black; tail chestnut.

Soft Parts: Bill yellow with red base; iris brown; orbital skin red; feet dark red.

Measurements: Wing ♂ 202, ♀ 193; tail ♂ 107, ♀ 104; bill 26; tarsus 39.

Range: Western Samoa (Savaii, Upolu)

Remarks: Found in original forest, although it may be seen near towns, this secretive bird lives between 1000-4500 feet and is most often found sitting on large limbs near tree trunks in shaded areas. The nest is well hidden in thick foliage about 15-35 feet above the ground.

MANY-COLORED FRUIT DOVE PLATE 15

Ptilinopus perousii perousii Peale, 1848

1848 *Ptilinopus perousii* Peale, U. S. Expl. Expd., **8**:195 (Upolu, Samoa)
1855 *Kurukuru samoensis* Des Murs and Prevost, Voy. "Venus," Zool., p. 247
(Samoa)

Description: Male—forehead and crown magenta; chin, throat, face, and hind neck yellowish white; a wide magenta bar across upper mantle; back, rump, and edges of wing-coverts greenish yellow; primaries and secondaries dark bronze-green; tail pearl gray; breast white with magenta bases to feathers; lower breast with a yellowish magenta bar; belly yellowish white; under tail-coverts magenta. Female—differs from male by having all upperparts, except crown, green; underparts more greenish gray. Immature—mostly green.
Soft Parts: Bill greenish; iris, male = red, female = yellow; feet gray.
Measurements: Wing ♂ 138, ♀ 130; tail ♂ 84, ♀ 79; bill 11; tarsus 21.
Range: American Samoa (Ofu, Olosega, Tau, Tutuila)
Western Samoa (Apolima, Savaii, Upolu)

Ptilinopus perousii mariae (Jacquinot and Pucheran, 1853)

1853 *Ptinilopus* [sic] *mariae* Jacquinot and Pucheran, Voy. Pole Sud, Zool.,
3:115 (Balaou = Ovalau, Fiji)
1864 *Ptilinopus caesarinus* Hartlaub, Journ. f. Orn., **12**:413 (Viti Levu)
1925 *Ptilinopus perousii cupidineus* Wetmore, Ibis, p. 829 (Tongatabu, Tonga)

Description: Differs from *P. p. perousii* as follows: Male—white areas of underparts purer white. Female—under tail-coverts yellow.
Range: Fiji (Aiwa, Fulanga, Kambara, Kandavu, Katafanga, Kio, Lakemba, Makongai, Mango, Mothe, Munia, Naitaumba, Namuka, Nayau, Olorua, Oneata, Ongea Levu, Taveuni, Thikombia-I-Lau, Totoya, Vanua Levu, Vanuambalavu, Vanuavatu, Vatoa, Vatulele, Viti Levu, Wakaya, Yandua, Yangasalevu, Yangganga, Yathata)
Tonga (Eua, Late, Tofua, Tongatapu)

Remarks: A bird of the deep forest, this dove is most active during the early morning hours when it feeds in tree tops.

74

PLATE 15

A MANY-COLORED FRUIT DOVE
   (*Ptilinopus perousii mariae*), male—page 73

B MANY-COLORED FRUIT DOVE
   (*Ptilinopus perousii mariae*), female—page 73

C RAROTONGAN FRUIT DOVE
   (*Ptilinopus rarotongensis rarotongensis*), female—page 77

D CRIMSON-CROWNED FRUIT DOVE
   (*Ptilinopus porphyraceus porphyraceus*), male—page 76

E GRAY-GREEN FRUIT DOVE
   (*Ptilinopus purpuratus chrysogaster*), male—page 78

F GRAY-GREEN FRUIT DOVE
   (*Ptilinopus purpuratus insularis*), male—page 79

G GRAY-GREEN FRUIT DOVE
   (*Ptilinopus purpuratus purpuratus*), male—page 78

H RAPA ISLAND FRUIT DOVE
   (*Ptilinopus huttoni*), male—page 80

PLATE 15

SANDSTRÖM

CRIMSON-CROWNED FRUIT DOVE   PLATE 15

Ptilinopus porphyraceus porphyraceus (Temminck, 1821)

1821   *Columba porphyracea* Temminck, Trans. Linn. Soc. London, **13**:130 (Tongatabu, Ulieta, and Timor = Tongatubu)

1826   *Columba forsteri* Desmarest, Dict. Sci. Nat., ed. Levrault, **40**:340 (new name for *Columba porphyracea* Temminck, 1841)

1835   *Columba viridissima* Temminck, Pl. Col., livr. 95, pl. 2 (Tongatabu)

1853   *Ptilopus clementinae* Jacquinot and Pucheran, Voy. Pole Sud, Zool., **3**:117 (Viti, Fiji)

1859   *Columba tabuensis* G. R. Gray (ex Latham), Cat. Bds. Trop. Isl. Pac., p. 38

1870   *Ptilopus bonapartei* G. R. Gray, Hand. Gen. Bds. Brit. Mus., **2**:225 (Vanikoro = Ovalau, Fiji)

1877   *Ptilonopus whitmeei* Ramsay, Proc. Linn. Soc. New South Wales, **2**:141 (Savage Island = Niue)

Description: Forehead and crown bright purple; hind neck and upper back gray-green; back, rump, and wing-coverts green; primaries, secondaries, and tail dark green with a glossy blue-green metallic wash; rectrices tipped with grayish white; chin whitish; throat and breast gray; breast dark green with a dark purplish patch in the center; lower breast and vent yellow; under tail-coverts orangish yellow.

Soft Parts: Bill green; iris yellow; feet red.

Measurements: Wing ♂ 140, ♀ 136; tail ♂ 80, ♀ 75; bill 17; tarsus 22.

Range: Fiji (Aiwa, Avea, Fulanga, Kambara, Katafanga, Komo, Lakemba, Makongai, Mango, Marambo, Mothe, Munia, Naitaumba, Namenalala, Namuka-I-Lau, Nayau, Nggele Levu, Nukumbasanga, Oneata, Ongea Levu, Thikombia-I-Lau, Thithia, Thombia, Tuvutha, Vanuavatu, Vatulele, Vatuvara, Wakaya, Wanggava, Watanua, Welangilala, Yandua, Yangasalevu, Yanutha, Yathata)

Nive

Rotuma

Tonga (Ava, Eua, Foa, Haafeva, Haano, Hunga Haapai, Hunga Tonga, Kao, Kapa, Late, Moungaone, Niuatoputapu, Nomuka, Ofolanga, Ovaka, Tafahi, Telekivavau, Tofua, Tongatapu, Tungua, Uiha, Uoleva, Vavau)

Ptilinopus porphyraceus fasciatus Peale, 1848

1848   *Ptilinopus fasciatus* Peale, U. S. Expl. Expd., **8**:193 (Samoan Islands)

1855   *Ptilinopus apicalis* Bonaparte, "C.G.A.," **2**:23 (Vavau; error = Samoa)

1878   *Ptilopus pictiventris* Elliot, Ann. Mag. Nat. Hist., p. 349 (Navigator and Friendly Islands)

Description: Differs from *P. p. porphyraceus* by having the rectrices tipped with yellowish white, the patch in the middle of the belly reddish brown, and the orange in the yellow under tail-coverts much more pronounced.
Range: American Samoa (Ofu, Olosega, Tau, Tutuila)
        Western Samoa (Savaii, Upolu)

Ptilinopus porphyraceus graeffei Neumann, 1922

1922   *Ptilinopus porphyraceus graeffei* Neumann, Ver. Orn. Ges. Bayern, **15**:234
        (Uvea or Wallis Island)

Description: This form is intermediate between *P. p. porphyraceus* and *fasciatus.* The reddish brown of the belly and the orange in the under tail-coverts are not quite as intense as in *fasciatus* but are distinctly different from *P. p. porphyraceus* and *fasciatus.*
Range: Horne Islands (Futuna, Uvea)
        Tonga (Niuafoo)

Remarks: Although a common bird of the scrub and plantations, this bird prefers the tops of forest fruit trees. Its mournful call can be heard at any time of the day.

RAROTONGAN FRUIT DOVE   PLATE 15

Ptilinopus rarotongensis rarotongensis Hartlaub and Finsch, 1871

1871   *Ptilinopus rarotongensis* Hartlaub and Finsch, Proc. Zool. Soc. London,
        p. 30 (Rarotonga)

Description: Forehead and crown purple; face and hind neck gray; back, rump, and wing-coverts dull green; primaries dark olive-black with narrow yellow margins; secondaries greenish with broad yellowish margins; tail green with a gray terminal band; chin and throat cream color; upper breast gray; lower breast dark olive-yellow with a maroon patch in the center; belly and under tail-coverts yellow; thighs grayish green. Immature—forehead and underparts paler.
Soft Parts: Bill plumbeous; iris yellow; feet reddish brown.
Measurements: Wing ♀ 130, ♂ 132; tail ♀ 85, ♂ 91; bill 14; tarsus 21.
Range: Cook Islands (Rarotonga)

Ptilinopus rarotongensis goodwini Holyoak, 1974

1974   *Ptilinopus rarotongensis goodwini* Holyoak, Bull. Brit. Orn. Cl., **94**:145
        (Atiu, Cook Islands)

Description: Differs from *P. r. rarotongensis* by having the red-maroon patch in the center of the belly reduced to a few feathers with orange tips.
Range: Cook Islands (Atiu)

Remarks: This bird is common in trees, but otherwise its habits are unknown.

GRAY-GREEN FRUIT DOVE   PLATE 15

Ptilinopus purpuratus purpuratus (Gmelin, 1789)

1789   *Columba purpurata* Gmelin, Syst. Nat., **1**:784 ("In insulis australis intra tropicos inclusis" = Tahiti)
1828   *Columba Kurukuru* var. *taitensis* Lesson, Voy. "Coquille," p. 297 (Tahiti)
1829   *Columba oopa* Wagler, Isis, **7**, col. 742 (Society Islands)
1848   *Ptilinopus furcatus* Peale, U. S. Expl. Expd., **8**:191 (Tahiti)
1855   *Kurukuru nebrouxii* Des Murs and Prevost, Voy. "Venus," Zool., p. 253 (Tahiti)

Description: Male—forehead and crown pale grayish purple; hind neck grayish; rest of upperparts green; primaries blackish with dark green margins; tail green with an indistinct subterminal gray band; chin dirty white; throat and breast grayish; belly grayish with a green wash; under tail-coverts yellow. Female—upperparts washed with bronze.
Soft Parts: Bill greenish yellow, nostrils orange; iris orange; feet red.
Measurements: Wing ♂ 150, ♀ 147; tail ♂ 87, ♀ 83; bill 11; tarsus 29.
Range: Society Islands (Tahiti)

Ptilinopus purpuratus frater Ripley and Birckhead, 1942

1942   *Ptilinopus purpuratus frater* Ripley and Birckhead, Am. Mus. Novit., 1192:9 (Moorea, Society Islands)

Description: Differs from *P. p. purpuratus* by having the upperparts slightly more brownish green and the gray of the underparts brighter.
Range: Society Islands (Moorea)

Ptilinopus purpuratus chrysogaster (G. R. Gray, 1853)

1853   *Ptilonopus chrysogaster* G. R. Gray, (1854), Proc. Zool. Soc. London, p. 48 (Raiatea, Society Islands)

Description: Differs from *P. p. purpuratus* by having the crown purer lavender with a distinct yellowish green hind border, the green of the upperparts brighter, the tail band distinctly terminal, the chin yellowish, upper breast olive-yellow, and lower breast and belly yellow.
Range: Society Islands (Bora-Bora, Huahine, Raiatea, Tahaa)

Ptilinopus purpuratus coralensis Peale, 1848

1848 *Ptilinopus coralensis* Peale, U. S. Expl. Expd., **8**:190 (Aratika, Tuamotu Group)

1893 *Ptilopus smithsonianus* Salvadori, Cat. Bds. Brit. Mus., **21**:105 ("Some island of the Paumotu Group")

Description: Differs from *P. p. chrysogaster* by having the forehead gray, the green of the upperparts not so bright, the chin whitish, the upper breast more yellow-gray, and the lower breast and under tail-coverts light whitish yellow.
Range: Tuamotu Archipelago (Ahe, Apataki, Aratika, Arutua, Faaite, Fakarava, Hiti, Katiu, Kauehi, Makemo, Manihi, Marutea, Maturei-Vavao, Niau, Rangiroa, Raraka, Taenga, Tahanea, Taiaro, Takaroa, Tenararo, Tenaruga, Tepoto, Tikehau, Toau, Tuanake)

Ptilinopus purpuratus chalcurus (G. R. Gray, 1859)

1859 *Ptilonopus chalcurus* G. R. Gray, Cat. Bds. Trop. Isl. Pac., p. 37 (Makatea Island, Paumotu Group)

Description: Differs from *P. p. coralensis* by having the crown magenta and the underparts more greenish.
Range: Tuamotu Archipelago (Makatea)

Ptilinopus purpuratus insularis (North, 1908)

1908 *Ptilopus insularis* North, Rec. Austral. Mus., **7**:30 (Henderson Island)

Description: Differs from *P. p. coralensis* by having the crown dark red; the upperparts more bronze, especially the tail; the throat and upper breast darker gray; and the lower belly purer white.
Range: Henderson Island

Remarks: This is a common dove of the original forest and forest edges. The birds on the smaller islands are much tamer than those of the larger, more populated ones. The birds on Tahiti are probably the shyest of all.

RAPA ISLAND FRUIT DOVE   PLATE 15

Ptilinopus huttoni (Finsch, 1874)

1874   *Ptilonopus huttoni* Finsch, Proc. Zool. Soc. London, p. 92 (Rapa Island)

Description: Forehead and crown lavender; hind neck gray-green; rest of upperparts green; wings and tail dark glossy green; chin very pale lavender; throat and upper breast greenish gray; lower breast and belly purple; lower belly and vent yellow; thighs gray; under tail-coverts reddish purple.

Soft Parts: Bill red with yellow tip; iris orange; feet red, slightly more orangish in immatures.

Measurements: Wing ♂ 169, ♀ 165; tail ♂ 118, ♀ 115; bill 21; tarsus 29.

Range: Austral Islands (Rapa)

Remarks: Nothing is recorded of this bird's habits.

WHITE-CAPPED FRUIT DOVE   PLATE 16

Ptilinopus dupetithouarsii dupetithouarsii (Neboux, 1840)

1840   *Columba Du Petithouarsii* Neboux, Rev. Zool., p. 289 (Tahuata, Marquesas)

Description: Forehead and crown white; yellow spot over eye and narrow orange fringe to hind crown; hind neck gray-green; rest of upperparts dull olive-green; wings dark green; inner secondaries dark glossy blue-green; tail bright green with a white tip; chin whitish; throat and upper breast gray washed with green; center of breast reddish orange; lower breast, vent, and under tail-coverts yellow. Immature—differs by lacking white crown and being generally duller.

Soft Parts: Bill, base maroon, tip blue-green; iris gray to olive-brown; feet coral red.

Measurements: Wing 144; tail 78; bill 12; tarsus 26.

Range: Marquesas Islands (Fatu Hiva, Hiva Oa, Motane, Tahuata)

Ptilinopus dupetithouarsii viridior (Murphy, 1924)

1924   *Ptilopus dupetithouarsi viridior* Murphy, Am. Mus. Novit., 115:4 (Nuku-hiva, Marquesas)

Description: Differs from *P. d. dupetithouarsii* by having the hind neck, face, chin, throat, and upper breast paler gray washed with light yellow-green; under tail-coverts in series paler yellow.

Range: Marquesas Islands (Nuku Hiva, Ua Huka, Ua Pu)

Remarks: A common dove of the tree tops, it can be found at most any altitude throughout its range.

RED-MOUSTACHED FRUIT DOVE   PLATE 16

Ptilinopus mercierii tristrami (Salvadori, 1892)

1892   *Ptilopus tristrami* Salvadori, Bull. Mus. Zool. Anat. Comp. Univ. Torino, 7:1 (Hivaoa Island, Marquesas Group)

Description: Forehead, crown, and moustache purplish red; an orange-yellow band runs from over the eye around behind the crown to the other eye; hind neck, upper back, throat, and breast gray; chin dirty white; back, rump, and wing-coverts olive-green; wings dark green; tail dark green with gray-white tips to rectrices; belly and under tail-coverts dark yellow; thighs gray.
Soft Parts: Bill, base and nostrils maroon, middle bluish, tip pea green; iris yellow, orbital ring red; feet dark purplish red.
Measurements: Wing ♂ 140, ♀ 136; tail ♂ 82, ♀ 80; bill 18; tarsus 26.
Range: Marquesas Islands (Hiva Oa)

Ptilinopus mercierii mercierii (Des Murs and Prevost, 1849)

1849   *Kurukuru Mercierii* Des Murs and Prevost, Voy. "Venus," Zool., p. 266 (Valley of Mohana, Nukuhiva Island, Marquesas)

Description: Differs from *P. m. tristrami* by having the purplish red of the crown more extensive and lacking the orange-yellow band around behind the crown.
Range: Marquesas Islands (Nuku Hiva). May be extinct.

Remarks: Little is known of this species; the nominate race, *P. m. mercierii,* has not been seen in this century, although several parties have searched for it.

ORANGE DOVE   PLATE 16

Ptilinopus victor victor (Gould, 1872)

1872   *Chrysoena victor* Gould, (1871), Proc. Zool. Soc. London, p. 642 (Bua, Fiji = M'Bua in southwest part of Vanua Levu)

Description: Male—head and chin dark greenish yellow; rest of upper-parts bright reddish orange; wings grayish yellow; rectrices grayish yellow with orange tips; underparts bright orange. Female—head and chin

dark olive-yellow; rest of bird dark green except under tail-coverts, which are dark yellow. Immature—similar to female but feathers have yellow margins.
Soft Parts: Bill green; iris yellow; feet greenish.
Measurements: Wing ♂ 120, ♀ 119; tail ♂ 62, ♀ 62; bill 14; tarsus 21.
Range: Fiji (Kio, Lauthala, Rambi, Taveuni, Vanua Levu, Viti Levu)

Ptilinopus victor aureus Amadon, 1943

1943   *Ptilinopus victor aureus* Amadon, Am. Mus. Novit., 1237:7 (Ngamea, Fiji)

Description: Differs from *P. v. victor* as follows: Males—upperparts brighter orange like underparts. Females—brighter underparts. Also larger: wing ♂ 127, ♀ 124; tail 68.
Range: Fiji (Nggamea)

Remarks: Nothing has been recorded with reference to the habits of this bird other than that it eats berries and fruits.

GOLDEN DOVE   PLATE 16

Ptilinopus luteovirens (Hombron and Jacquinot, 1841)

1841   *Columba luteovirens* Hombron and Jacquinot, Ann. Sci. Nat., **16**:315 (Balaou = Ovalau, Fiji)
1841   *Columba felicia* Hombron and Jacquinot, Ann. Sci. Nat., **16**:316 (Viti) [juv. of above]
1844   *Columba flava* G. R. Gray, Gen. Bds., **2**:470 (Viti)
1855   *Chrysoena lutea* Bonaparte, Consp. Av., **2**:28 (Fiji)

Description: Male—head and chin dark greenish yellow with a yellowish posterior band; back, rump, wing-coverts, throat, and breast feathers narrow and pointed in shape, outermost golden green with bases blackish, giving a grasslike appearance; primaries and secondaries gray-green with yellow margins; tail green; lower breast and under tail-coverts golden yellow; thighs green mottled with yellow. Female—upperparts uniformly dark green; underparts lighter green; feathers of breast, belly, and under tail-coverts have yellow margins.
Soft Parts: Bill green; iris yellow; feet green.
Measurements: Wing ♂ 120, ♀ 119; tail 68; bill 16; tarsus 19.
Range: Fiji (Mbengga, Ngau, Ovalau, Viti Levu, Waya)

Remarks: A well-camouflaged bird of the dense original forest, it is usually found in tree tops but also may be found in the second story.

VELVET DOVE PLATE 16

Ptilinopus layardi (Elliot, 1878)

1875 *Chrysoena viridis* Layard, Proc. Zool. Soc. London, p. 151 (Kandavu, Fiji Islands)

1878 *Ptilopus layardi* Elliot, Proc. Zool. Soc. London, p. 567 (new name for *Chrysoena viridis* Layard, 1875; not *Columba viridis* Linne, 1766)

Description: Male—head, including chin and upper throat, greenish yellow; rest of bird dark green except for rump, primaries, secondaries, and tail, which are brighter green; lower belly grayish; under tail-coverts yellow. Female—differs from male by having head, chin, and upper throat green; under tail-coverts paler yellow.

Soft Parts: Bill green; iris yellow-gray; feet reddish.

Measurements: Wing ♂ 118, ♀ 116; tail 55; bill 18; tarsus 23.

Range: Fiji (Kandavu, Ono)

Remarks: Nothing has been recorded with reference to this bird's habits.

PACIFIC PIGEON PLATE 17

Ducula pacifica pacifica (Gmelin, 1789)

1789 *Columba pacifica* Gmelin, Syst. Nat., **1**:777 (Insulis Amicis = Tonga Islands)

1829 *Columba globicera* Wagler, Isis, **7**:738 (Tonga Islands)

1855 *Globicera microcera* Bonaparte, Compt. Rend. Acad. Sci. Paris, **40**:215 (Vavau and Samoa)

1914 *Globicera pacifica queenslandica* Mathews, Austr. Av. Rec., **2**:84 (Mackay, Queensland; error = Tonga Islands)

1923 *Ducula pacifica intensitincta* "Neumann" Stresemann, Arch. f. Natürg., **89**A:76 (Fiji Islands)

Description: Top of head, hind neck, and upper back gray; back, rump, wings, and tail dark glossy blue-green; chin pale gray; breast gray; belly vinaceous; under tail-coverts dark chestnut.

Soft Parts: Bill black; iris red (brownish in young birds); feet orange-red.

Measurements: Wing 225; tail 148; bill 25; tarsus 32.

Range: Found on all the islands, even small islets, throughout Fiji, Niue, the Samoas, and Tonga to the Solomons.

Remarks: This large forest pigeon is rather wary and lives in the primary and secondary growth of the forest at most any altitude. It seems to favor the tops of dead trees or dead limbs.

SOCIETY ISLANDS PIGEON   PLATE 17

Ducula aurorae (Peale, 1848)

1848 *Carpophaga aurorae* Peale, U. S. Expl. Expd., **8**:201 (Makatea Island, Tuamotu Group)

1848 *Carpophaga wilkesii* Peale, U. S. Expl. Expd., **8**:203 (Tahiti)

Description: Forehead whitish; head, hind neck, and upper back gray; rest of upperparts black glossed with green; underparts gray.
Soft Parts: Bill black; iris crimson; feet coral-red.
Measurements: Wing ♂ 272, ♀ 260; tail 175; bill 26; tarsus 34.
Range: Society Islands (Tahiti)
          Tuamotu Archipelago (Makatea)

Remarks: This is a shy pigeon of the dense forest. Its call is a deep owl-like "hooo hooo," and it has a small casque on its bill.

MARQUESAS PIGEON   PLATE 17

Ducula galeata (Bonaparte, 1855)

1855 *Serresius galeatus* Bonaparte, Compt. Rend. Acad. Sci. Paris, **41**:1110 (western part of the Island of Nukuhiva, Marquesas Islands)

Description: Forehead dirty white; crown, hind neck, and upper back dark gray; back, rump, and wing-coverts dark glossy green; primaries black; tail black glossed with green; underparts gray, thighs darker; under tail-coverts chestnut.
Soft Parts: Bill black; iris white; feet dark maroon.
Measurements: Wing ♂ 310, ♀ 296; tail ♂ 235, ♀ 224; bill 39; tarsus ♂ 43, ♀ 35.
Range: Marquesas Islands (Nuku Hiva)

Remarks: A bird of the original forest, this pigeon is found feeding in fruit trees on the western end of the island above 2000 feet. It has a large casque on its bill.

PEALE'S PIGEON   PLATE 17

Ducula latrans (Peale, 1848)

1848   *Carpophaga latrans* Peale, U. S. Expl. Expd., **8**:200 (Fiji Islands)
1854   *Carpophaga ochropygia* Bonaparte, Compt. Rend. Acad. Sci. Paris, **39**:1074 (Balaou)

Description: Head, neck, and upper back gray; back, rump, and wings brownish gray; tail dull chestnut-brown; chin whitish; throat and breast pinkish gray; belly rufous; under tail-coverts cream washed with rufous.
Soft Parts: Bill black; iris red; feet reddish.
Measurements: Wing ♂ 223–252, ♀ 225–238; tail 175; bill 29; tarsus 34.
Range: Fiji (Avea, Kanathea, Kandavu, Koro, Mango, Matuku, Moala, Mokongai, Naitaumba, Nayau Ngau, Ovalau, Rambi, Taveuni, Thikombia, Thithia, Totoya, Tuvutha, Vanua Levu, Vanuambalavu, Vatuvara, Viti Levu, Wakaya)

Remarks: A pigeon of the dense original forest, it may be found near the ground as well as in tree tops.

PSITTACIDAE   PARROTS

COLLARED LORY   PLATE 18

Phigys solitarius (Suckow, 1800)

1800   *Psittacus solitarius* Suckow, Anf. Theor. ang. Naturg. Thier, **2**:334 (Fiji Islands)
1810   *Psittacus vaillanti* Shaw, Nat. Misc., **21**, pl. 909 (Southern Islands = Fiji)
1811   *Psittacus coccineus* Shaw, Gen. Zool., **8**:472 (no locality = Fiji)
1811   *Psittacus phigy* Bechstein, Kurze Uebers., suppl., p. 81 (Fiji)

Description: Top of head and crest very dark purple; hind collar bright green; upper back crimson; central back and wings green; rump and upper tail-coverts bright green; tail green, the two central rectrices having a central orange spot and the other rectrices having a dark reddish spot on the inner margin; chin, throat, breast, and upper belly crimson; lower belly and thighs purple; under tail-coverts bright green. Immature—breast feathers tipped with purple.
Soft Parts: Bill yellow; iris orange-brown; feet yellowish.
Measurements: Wing ♂ 136, ♀ 131; tail ♂ 65, ♀ 63; bill 16; tarsus 14.

Range: Fiji (Kandavu, Lakemba, Leleuvia, Matuku, Nukulau, Oneata, Ono, Rambi, Taveuni, Tuvutha, Vanua Levu, Vatuvara, Viti Levu, Wakaya, Yathata)

Remarks: A bird of the lowlands, it is usually found in coconut plantations and around flowering trees of the native forest.

RED-THROATED LORIKEET   PLATE 18

Charmosyna amabilis (Ramsay, 1876)

1875   *Trichoglossus aureocinctus* Layard, Ann. Mag. Nat. Hist., **16**:344 (Fiji Islands)

1876   *Trichoglossus (Glossopsitta) amabilis* Ramsay, Proc. Linn. Soc. New South Wales, **1**:30 (Ovalau, Fiji)

Description: Upperparts green; tail green above with yellow ends to rectrices; lores, cheeks, and throat red; narrow band between throat and breast yellow; breast, belly, and under tail-coverts green; thighs reddish maroon; under surface of tail yellowish. Immature—similar to adults but generally greener, especially the breast bands and under tail surface.
Soft Parts: Bill orange; iris yellow; feet orange.
Measurements: Wing ♂ 94, ♀ 93; tail ♂ 78, ♀ 79; bill 10; tarsus 12.
Range: Fiji (Ovalau, Taveuni, Viti Levu)

Remarks: This little-known and well-camouflaged bird is usually found above 2000 feet feeding in the tops of flowering trees.

BLUE-CROWNED LORY   PLATE 18

Vini australis (Gmelin, 1788)

1788   *Psittacus australis* Gmelin, Syst. Nat., **1**:329 (Sandwich Islands; error = Samoa)

1788   *Psittacus fringillaceus* Gmelin, Syst. Nat., **1**:337 (South America; error = Samoa)

1789   *Psittacus porphyreocephalus* Shaw, Nat. Misc., **1**, pl. 1 (Islands of South Seas = Samoa)

1790   *Psittacus pipilans* Latham, Ind. Orn., **1**:105 (Sandwich Islands = Samoa)

1832   *Coriphilus euchlorus* Wagler, Mon. Psitt., p. 564 (Tongatabu, Friendly Islands)

Description: Forehead bright green; crown dark blue; hind collar green; back and wing-coverts dull brownish green; rump and upper tail-coverts bright green; primaries and secondaries blackish with outer margins green; tail, rectrices dark green tipped with dark golden yellow; chin and throat bright red; breast green; center of belly bright red; lower belly and vent dark purplish red; flanks and under tail-coverts bright green. Immature—less red on face, throat, and abdomen.

Soft Parts: Bill orange-red; iris light yellow-brown; feet orange-red.

Measurements: Wing ♂ 111, ♀ 109; tail ♂ 66, ♀ 64; bill 14; tarsus 13.

Range: American Samoa (Ofu, Olosega, Tau)
Fiji (Fulanga, Mothe, Oneata, Ongea Levu, Vatoa)
Horne Islands (Alofi, Futuna)
Niue
Tonga (Eua, Fotuhaa, Haafeva, Haapai Group, Niuafoo, Niuatoputapu, Tafahi, Tofua, Tongatapu, Tungua, Uiha, Uoleva, Vavau)
Wallis
Western Samoa (Apolima, Manono, Savaii, Upolu)

Remarks: A common bird, often seen in large flocks, it ranges from seacoast to mountain tops but is found mostly around flowering trees, especially in or near coconut plantations.

RIMATARA LORIKEET   PLATE 18

Vini kuhlii (Vigors, 1824)

1824 *Psittacula Kuhlii* Vigors, Zool. Journ., 1:412 (Toohooteterooha Island. A day's sail from Otaheite)

1831 *Vini coccinea* Lesson, Illus. Zool., pl. 28 (Society Islands)

Description: Forehead and crown bright green; crest feathers of hind crown dark purplish; hind neck dark green; upper back brownish green; lower back and rump light green; wing-coverts and outer margins of primaries bluish green, with rest of primaries blackish brown; tail, rectrices mostly red with blackish bases and terminated with green; chin, throat, breast, and upper belly bright crimson; lower belly and thighs dark purplish red; under tail-coverts light green. Immature—similar to adults but underparts are mottled with green and the green tips of the rectrices are smaller.

Soft Parts: Bill yellowish; iris reddish yellow; feet orange-yellow.

Measurements: Wing ♂ 134, ♀ 129; tail ♂ 70, ♀ 69; bill 15; tarsus 14.

Range: Austral Islands (Rimatara)

Remarks: This bird is usually found in coconut plantations but also likes the original forest of the mountains; it travels in small flocks.

88

PLATE 16

A WHITE-CAPPED FRUIT DOVE
(*Ptilinopus dupetithouarsii dupetithouarsii*), male—page 80

B RED-MOUSTACHED FRUIT DOVE
(*Ptilinopus mercierii tristrami*), male—page 81

C ORANGE DOVE
(*Ptilinopus victor victor*), male—page 81

D ORANGE DOVE
(*Ptilinopus victor victor*), female—page 81

E GOLDEN DOVE
(*Ptilinopus luteovirens*), male—page 82

F GOLDEN DOVE
(*Ptilinopus luteovirens*), female—page 82

G VELVET DOVE
(*Ptilinopus layardi*), male—page 83

H VELVET DOVE
(*Ptilinopus layardi*), female—page 83

PLATE 16

90

PLATE 17

A   MARQUESAS PIGEON
    (*Ducula galeata*), male—page 84

B   PEALE'S PIGEON
    (*Ducula latrans*), male—page 85

C   SOCIETY ISLANDS PIGEON
    (*Ducula aurorae*), male—page 84

D   PACIFIC PIGEON
    (*Ducula pacifica*), male—page 83

E   ROCK DOVE
    (*Columba livia*), male—page 66

F   WHITE-THROATED PIGEON
    (*Columba vitiensis vitiensis*), male—page 66

G   WHITE-THROATED PIGEON
    (*Columba vitiensis castaneiceps*), male—page 67

SANDSTRÖM

PLATE 17

PLATE 18

A   COLLARED LORY
    (*Phigys solitarius*), male—page 85

B   RED-THROATED LORIKEET
    (*Charmosyna amabilis*), male—page 86

C   RIMATARA LORIKEET
    (*Vini kuhlii*), male—page 87

D   BLUE-CROWNED LORY
    (*Vini australis*), male—page 86

E   MARQUESAS LORIKEET
    (*Vini ultramarina*), male—page 95

F   HENDERSON ISLAND LORIKEET
    (*Vini stepheni*), male—page 94

G   PACIFIC LORIKEET
    (*Vini peruviana*), male—page 94

PLATE 18

HENDERSON ISLAND LORIKEET   PLATE 18

Vini stepheni (North, 1908)

1908   *Calliptilus* (?) *stepheni* North, Rec. Austral. Mus., **7**:29 (Henderson Island)
1913   *Vini hendersoni* Ogilvie-Grant, Bull. Brit. Orn. Cl., **31**:60 (Henderson Island)

Description: Forehead and crown bright green; back and wing-coverts brownish green; primaries blackish with green outer margins; lower back, rump, and upper tail-coverts light green; tail yellow-green with outer rectrices having a red spot near the base on the inner margin; chin, throat, breast, and upper belly crimson with a greenish purple breast band; lower belly and thighs dark purplish red; under tail-coverts bright green.
Soft Parts: Bill yellowish; iris yellow; feet yellow-orange.
Measurements: Wing ♂ 129, ♀ 126; tail ♂ 90, ♀ 88; bill 13; tarsus 14.
Range: Henderson Island

Remarks: The habits of this bird are unknown.

PACIFIC LORIKEET   PLATE 18

Vini peruviana (P. L. S. Müller, 1776)

1776   *Psittacus peruvianus* P. L. S. Müller, Natursyst., suppl., 1776:80 (Peru = Tahiti)
1787   *Psittacus cyaneus* Sparrman, Mus. Carls., pl. 27 (Tahiti)
1788   *Psittacus taitianus* Gmelin, Syst. Nat., p. 329 (Tahiti)
1788   *Psittacus varius* Gmelin, Syst. Nat., p. 337 (South America; error = Tahiti)
1789   *Psittacus porphyrio* Shaw and Nodder, Nat. Misc., **1**, pl. 7 (Tahiti)
1811   *Psittacus sparmanni* Bechstein, Kurze Uebers, suppl., p. 80 (Tahiti)
1830   *Lorius vini* Lesson, Traite d' Orn., p. 194 (Tahiti)
1832   *Coriphilus sapphirinus* Wagler, Mon. Psitt., p. 563 (Tahiti)
1907   *Coriphilus cyaneus* S. B. Wilson, Ibis, p. 379 (Borabora)
1907   *Coriphilus cyanescens* S. B. Wilson, Ibis, p. 653 (new name for *Coriphilus cyaneus* S. B. Wilson, 1907; not *Psittacus cyaneus* Sparrman, 1787)

Description: Top of head, back, rump, and wing-coverts dark blue; primaries and rectrices blackish; chin, throat, and upper breast white; rest of underparts dark bluish black. Immature—differs from adult by having the underparts uniformly grayish black.
Soft Parts: Bill orange; iris light brown; feet orange.

Measurements: Wing ♂ 112, ♀ 110; tail ♂ 68, ♀ 67; bill 13; tarsus 13.
Range: Cook Islands (Aitutaki—possibly introduced)
Society Islands (Bora-Bora, Moorea, Scilly, Tahiti)
Tuamotu Archipelago (Apataki, Arutua, Kaukura, Rangiroa, Tikehau)

Remarks: Now restricted in its range to the Tuamotu Archipelago, this bird may be found in coconut plantations but is most common in the remaining original forests.

MARQUESAS LORIKEET   PLATE 18

Vini ultramarina (Kuhl, 1820)

1820 *Psittacus ultramarinus* Kuhl, Nova Acta Acad. Caes. Leop. Carol., **10**:49 (New Holland = Marquesas)

1841 *Psittaculus smaragdinus* Hombron and Jacquinot, Ann. Sci. Nat., **16**:318 (Marquesas)

1842 *Coryphilus dryas* Gould, Proc. Zool. Soc. London, p. 165 (Marquesas)

1843 *Psittacus ou Psittacula Lessoni* Lesson, Echo du Monde Sav., col. 924 (Nu-Kahiva = Nuku Hiva, Marquesas)

1853 *Coryphilus goupilii* Pucheran, Voy. Pole Sud, Zool., **3**:103 (Marquesas)

Description: Forehead bright ultramarine; crown and hind neck dark blue; back and wing-coverts ultramarine; rump and upper tail-coverts light ultramarine; primaries and secondaries blackish with outer margins dark ultramarine; tail white with outer margins pale ultramarine; chin and throat dark slate-blue with white-tipped feathers; breast band dark slate-blue; belly white with feathers having dark slate bases, giving a mottled appearance. Immature—similar to adult but lacks white on underparts.
Soft Parts: Bill, upper mandible yellow, lower mandible blackish; iris brownish yellow; feet brown.
Measurements: Wing ♂ 119, ♀ 117; tail ♂ 77, ♀ 74; bill 14; tarsus 13.
Range: Marquesas Islands (Nuku Hiva, Ua Pu)

Remarks: A bird of the original forest, it can be found feeding on flowering trees above 1500 feet.

RED-BREASTED MUSK PARROT   PLATE 19

Prosopeia tabuensis tabuensis (Gmelin, 1788)

1788   *Psittacus tabuensis* Gmelin, Syst. Nat., **1**:317 (Friendly Islands = Tonga)

1792   *Psittacus atropurpureus* Shaw, Mus. Lever., p. 140 (New Holland; error = Fiji)

1837–38   *Conurus Anna* Bourjot St. Hilaire, Hist. Nat. Perr., **3**, pl. 38 (Australasia)

Description: Forehead blackish maroon; crown and cheeks dark maroon; narrow blue collar; back, rump, and wing-coverts green; primaries and tail blue; chin blackish; throat, breast, belly, and under tail-coverts maroon.

Soft Parts: Bill black; iris orange; feet black.

Measurements: Wing ♂ 250, ♀ 236; tail ♂ 231, ♀ 230; bill ♂ 34, ♀ 28; tarsus ♂ 29, ♀ 27.

Range: Fiji (Ngau)
          Tonga (Eua, Tongatapu). Extinct.

Prosopeia tabuensis splendens (Peale, 1848)

1848   *Platycercus splendens* Peale, U. S. Expl. Expd., **8**:127 (Peale's River, Viti Levu, Fiji)

Description: Differs from *P. t. tabuensis* by having the forehead, cheeks, and crown crimson; the blue collar wider; and the underparts crimson. Also smaller.

Measurements: Wing ♂ 230, ♀ 220; tail ♂ 214, ♀ 213.

Range: Fiji (Kandavu; introduced on Viti Levu)

Prosopeia tabuensis atrogularis (Peale, 1848)

1848   *Platycercus atrogularis* Peale, U. S. Expl. Expd., **8**:129 (Feejee Islands = Vanua Levu)

Description: Differs from *P. t. tabuensis* by having the feathers at the base of the bill blackish and the blue collar wider and more conspicuous.

Range: Fiji (Kio, Vanua Levu)

Prosopeia tabuensis koroensis (Layard, 1876)

1876   *Platycercus koroensis* Layard, Ibis, p. 394 (Koro, Fiji Islands)

Description: Differs from *P. t. atrogularis* by lacking the blue collar and having the rump feathers tipped with maroon; differs from other races by having the maroon underparts darker.

Range: Fiji (Koro)

Prosopeia tabuensis taviunensis (Layard, 1876)

1876   *Platycercus taviunensis* Layard, Ibis, p. 141 (Taviuni, Fiji Islands)

Description: Differs from most races (i.e., except *P. t. koroensis*) by lacking the blue collar and from all races by its smaller size.
Measurements: Wing ♂ 224, ♀ 201; tail ♂ 194, ♀ 172.
Range: Fiji (Nggamea, Taveuni)

Remarks: A bird of the thick bush, it often feeds in fruit trees. It is found singly or in small flocks.

YELLOW-BREASTED MUSK PARROT   PLATE 19

Prosopeia personata (G. R. Gray, 1848)

1848   *Coracopsis* (?) *personata* G. R. Gray, Proc. Zool. Soc. London, p. 21 (New Guinea; error = Fiji)

Description: Forehead, cheeks, and chin black; upperparts green, with crown and rump brighter than the rest; primaries bluish; throat green; center of breast yellow; center of belly deep orange; flanks and under tail-coverts green.
Soft Parts: Bill black; iris orange; feet black.
Measurements: Wing ♂ 243, ♀ 229; tail ♂ 232, ♀ 224; bill ♂ 31, ♀ 26; tarsus ♂ 24, ♀ 23.
Range: Fiji (Viti Levu; formerly on Kandavu and Ovalau)

Remarks: A parrot of the underbrush and trees, this retiring bird may be found by its raucous call and its preference for original forest.

BLACK-FRONTED PARAKEET   PLATE 20

Cyanoramphus zealandicus (Latham, 1790)

1790   *Psittacus zealandicus* Latham, Ind. Orn., **1**:102 (New Zealand = Society Islands)

1820   *Psittacus erythronothus* Kuhl, Nova Acta Acad. Caes. Leop. Carol., **10**:45 (New Holland = Society Islands)

1845   *Conurus phaeton* Des Murs, Rev. Zool., p. 449 (Tahiti)

1868   *Cyanorhamphus forsteri* Finsch, Papag., **2**:270 (new name for *Psittacus erythronotus* Kuhl, 1820)

1897   *Cyanoramphus magnirostris* Forbes and Robinson, Bull. Liverpool Mus., **1**:21 (Tahiti, Society Islands)

Description: Forehead blackish brown; crown, back, and wing-coverts green; rump red; primaries blue-green, with outer web violet-blue; tail blue-green; lores and stripe behind eye red; underparts bluish green, somewhat darker on chin and throat.

Soft Parts: Bill bluish; iris unrecorded; feet gray-brown.

Measurements: Specimens unsexed average in wing 140; tail 139; bill 19; tarsus 25.

Range: Society Islands (Tahiti). Extinct.

Remarks: This bird has not been seen since 1844 and nothing is known of its habits; it was scarce when Captain Cook visited the islands in 1773.

SOCIETY PARAKEET   PLATE 20

Cyanoramphus ulietanus (Gmelin, 1788)

1788   *Psittacus ulietanus* Gmelin, Syst. Nat., **1**:328 (Ulietea, Society Islands)

Description: Head blackish brown; upper back and wing-coverts dark brownish green; lower back and rump red; tail-coverts green; tail olive-brown; underparts olive-yellow.

Soft Parts: Bill gray; iris unrecorded; feet gray-brown.

Measurements: Specimens unsexed average in wing 137; tail 132; bill 21; tarsus 23.

Range: Society Islands (Raiatea). Extinct.

Remarks: The habits of this bird are unknown. Two specimens were collected by Captain Cook in 1773, but none has been seen since that time.

CUCULIDAE   CUCKOOS

FAN-TAILED CUCKOO   PLATE 20

Cacomantis pyrrophanus simus (Peale, 1848)

1848   *Cuculus simus* Peale, U. S. Expl. Expd., **8**:134 (Sandalwood Bay, Fiji Islands)

1866   *Cuculus infuscatus* Hartlaub, Ibis, p. 172 (Viti Levu, Fiji)

Description: Upperparts gray with a strong greenish gloss; upper tail-coverts and tail blue-black, rectrices barred with white; underparts rufous.

Soft Parts: Bill, upper mandible black, lower mandible horn; iris brown; feet yellowish.

Measurements: Wing ♂ 127, ♀ 132; tail 131; bill 22; tarsus 23.

Range: Fiji (Kandavu, Makongai, Mathuata, Mbengga, Navandra, Ovalau, Taveuni, Vanua Kula, Vanua Levu, Vatu-I-Ra, Viti Levu, Wakaya, Yasawa)

Remarks: This is a common bird of the open country and forest edges.

LONG-TAILED CUCKOO PLATE 20

Eudynamys taitensis (Sparrman, 1787)

1787 *Cuculus taitensis* Sparrman, Mus. Carls., pl. 32 (no locality = Tahiti)

1788 *Cuculus tahitius* Gmelin, Syst. Nat., 1:412 (Tahiti)

1817 *Cuculus perlatus* Vieillot, Nouv. Dict. d'Hist. Nat., ed. 8, p. 232 (no locality = Tahiti, Society Islands)

1844 *Cuculus fasciatus* Forster, Descr. Anim., ed. Licht., p. 160 (Huaheine and Otaheiti = Tahiti)

1848 *Eudynamis cuneicauda* Peale, U. S. Expl. Expd., 8:139 (Ovalau, Fiji)

1917 *Urodynamis taitensis pheletes* Wetmore, Proc. Biol. Soc. Wash., **30**:1 (Otago Prov., New Zealand)

1918 *Urodynamis taitensis belli* Mathews, Bull. Brit. Orn. Cl., **29**:24 (Norfolk Island)

Description: Upperparts dark brown barred with rufous; superciliary stripe buffy white; chin and throat white washed with rufous and streaked dark brown on all sides; breast and belly white streaked with dark brown.

Soft Parts: Bill, upper mandible blackish, lower mandible horn whitish; iris orange-yellow; feet greenish.

Measurements: Wing ♂ 189, ♀ 181; tail ♂ 230, ♀ 215; bill 30; tarsus 33.

Range: Breeds in New Zealand and winters throughout the Central Pacific.

American Samoa (Aunuu, Manua Islands, Ofu, Olosega, Tau, Tutuila)

Austral Islands (Raevavae, Rapa, Rimatara, Tubuai, Varitao)

Cook Islands (Danger Atoll, Palmerston, Rarotonga)

Fiji (Luvuka, Mokani, Nakusemanu, Nanuku Levu, Ovalau, Taveuni, Vanuavatu, Vatoa, Viti Levu, Wakaya)

Horne Islands (Alofi, Futuna)
Marquesas Islands (Nuku Hiva)
Niue
Pitcairn Island
Society Islands (Bora-Bora, Huahine, Mehetia, Moorea, Raia-
    tea, Tahiti)
Tonga (Ata, Eua, Fonualei, Niuafoo, Nomuka, Tongatapu,
    Vavau)
Tuamotu Archipelago (Apataki, Hiti, Katiu, Magareva, Maka-
    tea, Makemo, Maria, Taiaro, Takahau, Takapoto, Takume,
    Tenaruga)
Wallis
Western Samoa (Savaii, Upolu)

Remarks: This is a migratory bird of the lowlands, most often seen in scrub but also found in low trees.

TYTONIDAE   BARN OWLS

BARN OWL   **PLATE 20**

Tyto alba lulu (Peale, 1848)

1848   *Strix lulu* Peale, U. S. Expl. Expd., **8**:74 ("Upolu and other islands of the
    Samoan group")

Description: Upperparts gray mottled with dark brown and burnt or-
ange; tail with four dark brown bars; face white with chestnut-brown
around eyes; underparts white spotted with black.
Soft Parts: Bill yellowish; iris black; feet yellowish brown.
Measurements: Wing 272; tail 112; bill 34; tarsus 64.
Range: American Samoa (Aunuu, Ofu, Olosega, Tau, Tutuila)
        Fiji (Aiwa, Kandavu, Ndravuni, Olorua, Ono-I-Lau, Taveuni,
            Vanua Kula, Vanua Levu, Vatulele, Viti Levu, Yasawa)
        Horne Islands (Futuna)
        Niue
        Rotuma
        Tonga (Haano, Hunga Haapai, Niuafoo, Nomuka, Telekiton-
            ga, Uiha, Uoleva)
        Western Samoa (Savaii, Upolu)

Remarks: The barn owl is common from seacoast to mountains. It is usually found from dusk to dawn in open areas where it hunts for mice. The loud, rasping, buglike call can be heard for some distance. Peters lists this bird from the Society Islands, but I know of no specimens from that locality.

GRASS OWL   PLATE 20

Tyto capensis walleri (Diggles, 1866)

1866   *Strix walleri* Diggles, Orn. Austr., pt. 7, pl. 14 (Brisbane, Queensland)

1879   *Strix oustaleti* Hartlaub, Proc. Zool. Soc. London, p. 295 (Wai-manu River, Viti Levu, Fiji Islands)

Description: Upperparts dark brown mottled with golden orange and spotted with white; tail golden orange with dark brown bars; underparts white, washed with ochre and spotted with dark brown.
Soft Parts: Bill pinkish white; iris blackish brown; feet gray-brown.
Measurements: Wing 357; tail 124; bill 39; tarsus 80.
Range: Fiji (Viti Levu)

Remarks: This is a rare owl of the grasslands; there are no recent records.

APODIDAE   SWIFTS

WHITE-RUMPED SWIFTLET   PLATE 22

Collocalia spodiopygia spodiopygia (Peale, 1848)

1848   *Macropteryx spodiopygius* Peale, U. S. Expl. Expd., **8**:176 (Upolu and Tutuila, Samoan Islands)

1854   *Herse forsteri* Hartlaub, Journ. f. Orn., **2**:169 (new name for *Hirundo peruviana* Forster, 1844)

Description: Upperparts dark brown washed with a greenish gloss and a whitish band across rump; underparts gray-brown.
Soft Parts: Bill black; iris brown; feet black.
Measurements: Wing 116; tail 50; bill 5; tarsus 8.
Range: American Samoa (Manua Islands, Tutuila)
              Western Samoa (Apolima, Savaii, Upolu)

PLATE 19

PLATE 19

PLATE 20

PLATE 20

SANDSTRÖM

Collocalia spodiopygia assimilis Stresemann, 1912

1912 *Collocalia francica assimilis* Stresemann, Nov. Zool., **19**:350 (Fiji Islands)
1918 *Zoonava francica oberholseri* Mathews, Bds. Austr., **7**:253 (Fiji Islands)

Description: Differs from *C. s. spodiopygia* by having the white of the rump reduced and less white, almost buffy.

Range: Fiji (Avea, Fulanga, Kambara, Kandavu, Katafanga, Koro, Lakemba, Mana, Mango, Matathawa Levu, Moala, Namukalau, Ndravuni, Niau, Oneata, Ongea Levu, Ono, Ovalau, Taveuni, Thikombia-I-Lau, Thithia, Tuvutha, Vatulele, Vawa, Viti Levu, Yathata)

Horne Islands (Futuna)

Collocalia spodiopygia townsendi Oberholser, 1906

1906 *Collocalia francica townsendi* Oberholser, Proc. Acad. Nat. Sci. Phila., **58**:197 (Eua Island, Tonga)

Description: Differs from *C. s. spodiopygia* by having the rump band more whitish.

Range: Niue

Tonga (Ava, Eua, Kao, Late, Niuafoo, Tofua, Vavau)

Remarks: This swiftlet is a common bird of the lowlands. It may be found flying around coconut trees, and it nests deep in caves.

TAHITI SWIFTLET   PLATE 22

Collocalia leucophaea leucophaea (Peale, 1848)

1848 *Macropteryx leucophaeus* Peale, U. S. Expl. Expd., **8**:178 (Tahiti)
1858 *Collocalia cinerea* Cassin, U. S. Expl. Expd., **8**:183 (Tahiti)
1906 *Collocalia thespesia* Oberholser. Proc. Acad. Nat. Sci. Phila., **58**:195 (Tahiti)
1974 *?Collocalia sawtelli* Holyoak, Bull. Brit. Orn. Cl., **94**:146 (Annataketake Cave, Atiu, Cook Islands). Morphologically indistinct (specimens examined) but alleged to differ from *C. l. leucocephala* by echo locating.

Description: Entire bird brown; underparts paler.
Soft Parts: Bill black; iris brown; feet pinkish brown.
Measurements: Wing 120; tail 60; bill 5; tarsus 10.
Range: Cook Islands (Atiu)
Society Islands (Moorea, Tahiti)

Collocalia leucophaea ocista Oberholser, 1906

1906 *Collocalia ocista* Oberholser, Proc. Acad. Nat. Sci. Phila., **58**:184 (Nuku-hiva, Marquesas Islands)

Description: Differs from *C. l. leucophaea* by being darker brown and having a metallic green wash on the upperparts.
Range: Marquesas Islands (Eiao, Hiva Oa, Nuku Hiva, Tahuata, Ua Huka, Ua Pu)

Remarks: A bird of the high mountains, it nests in caves and is most often seen during early morning and evening hours.

SPINE-TAILED SWIFT

Chaetura caudacuta (Latham, 1801)

1801 *Hirundo caudacuta* Latham, Ind. Orn., suppl., p. lvii (New South Wales)

Description: Top of head and upperparts light brown; tail and wings black with a green gloss; chin and throat white; breast and belly brown; under tail-coverts white tipped with brown.
Range: Fiji (Vatulele), as a migrant from Siberia

Remarks: The recent publication (March 1975) of a sight record from Fiji made it impossible to include this swift on a plate in this book. However, it is possible to list the species here. This Siberian migrant winters in Australia and New Zealand and should be looked for in other places in the southwest Pacific. Different subspecific identification will be determined when specimens are obtained.

ALCEDINIDAE   KINGFISHERS

FLAT-BILLED KINGFISHER   PLATE 21

Halcyon recurvirostris (Lafresnaye, 1842)

1842 *Todiramphus recurvirostris* Lafresnaye, Rev. Zool., p. 134 (In insulis maris Australis = Samoa)
1842 *Halcyon platyrostris* Gould, Proc. Zool. Soc. London, p. 72 (Navigators Islands)
1848 *Dacelo minima* Peale, U. S. Expl. Expd., **8**:159 (Upolu, Samoa)

Description: Male—upperparts bright greenish blue; primaries and rectrices somewhat darker; lores and superciliary spot buffy; ear-coverts blue-green; band on hind neck ochraceous-buff; chin, throat, and upper breast white; lower breast, flanks, and belly buff. Female—similar to male but upperparts duller. Immature—feathers of breast and hind neck edged with blackish.

Soft Parts: Bill, upper mandible black, lower mandible black with a white base; iris brown; feet black.

Measurements: Wing ♂ 80, ♀ 78; tail 64; bill 37.

Range: Western Samoa (Apolima, Savaii, Upolu)

Remarks: A common bird of the lowlands, it is usually found in pairs. The birds call to each other or in unison so that it sounds like one bird. It is most often found sitting on a dead limb.

WHITE-COLLARED KINGFISHER   PLATE 21

Halcyon chloris vitiensis (Peale, 1848)

1848 *Dacelo vitiensis* Peale, U. S. Expl. Expd., **8**:156 (Vanua Levu and Ovalau, Fiji Islands)

1867 *Halcyon cassini* Finsch and Hartlaub, Beitr. Fauna Cent., Orn., p. 40 (Ovalau)

1870 *Halcyon superciliosa* Gray, List Fissir. Brit. Mus., p. 56 (Fiji)

1892 *Halcyon suvensis* Sharpe, Cat. Bds. Brit. Mus., **17**:281 (Suva, Fiji)

Description: Male—top of head, back, and rump greenish blue; wings and tail blue; lores ochraceous; a white stripe runs from one eye, around behind the head, to the other eye, becoming more ochraceous at the nape; ear-coverts and collar beneath white stripe are blackish green; underparts white with light ochre wash on the flanks. Female—differs from the male by lacking the ochre on the lores, nape, and flanks and by having the ear-coverts darker.

Soft Parts: Bill blackish horn; iris brown; feet brownish.

Measurements: Wing ♂ 92, ♀ 99; tail ♂ 70, ♀ 74; bill 43; tarsus 14.

Range: Fiji (Koro, Ngau, Ovalau, Taveuni, Vanua Levu, Viti Levu)

Halcyon chloris marina Mayr, 1941

1941 *Halcyon chloris marina* Mayr, Am. Mus. Novit., 1152:2 (Ongea Levu, Fiji Islands)

Description: Differs from *H. c. vitiensis* by having the upperparts greener, loral spot larger, both collars broader, and underparts pure white. Also lacks the light ochre wash. Wing ♂ 95, ♀ 96.

Range: Fiji (Lau Archipelago)

Halcyon chloris eximia Mayr, 1941

1941   *Halcyon chloris eximia* Mayr, Am. Mus. Novit., 1152:2 (Ono Island, Fiji Islands)

Description: Differs from *H. c. marina* by having the upperparts bluer, ochre collar narrower, loral patch smaller, and hanks with a slight ochre wash in males; also larger (wing ♂ 99, ♀ 102).

Range: Fiji (Kandavu, Ndravuni, Ono, Vanua Kula, Yaukuve Levu)

Halcyon chloris sacra (Gmelin, 1788)

1788   *Alcedo sacra* Gmelin, Syst. Nat., **1**:453 (Society Islands, New Zealand, Philippines = Tongatabu, Tonga Islands)

1919   *Sauropatis sacra rabulata* Wetmore, Bull. Mus. Comp. Zool., **63**:197 (Eua, Tonga Islands)

1919   *Sauropatis sacra celada* Wetmore, Bull. Mus. Comp. Zool., **63**:198 (Vavau, Tonga Islands)

Description: Differs from *H. c. vitiensis* by having the upperparts much bluer, loral spot larger and whiter, white collar wider and whiter (less ochre), ear-coverts blue-green, and underparts white; also larger (wing ♂ 103, ♀ 106).

Range: Tonga (Ava, Eua, Foa, Fonoifua, Fotuhaa, Haafeva, Haano, Hunga, Hunga Haapai, Kao, Kelefesia, Late, Mango, Moungaone, Nomuka, Nomuka Iki, Ofolanga, Oua, Telekitonga, Tofua, Toku, Tongatapu, Tungua, Uiha, Uoleva, Vavau)

Halcyon chloris regina Mayr, 1941

1941   *Halcyon chloris regina* Mayr, Am. Mus. Novit., 1152:2 (Futuna Island, Central Polynesia)

Description: Male—top of head, back, and scapulars greenish; rump, tail, and primaries blue-green; lores and wide collar ochre, becoming quite dark at nape; cheeks and ear-coverts greenish black; underparts white with an ochre wash. Female—unknown.

Measurements: Wing ♂ 98; tail ♂ 64; bill ♂ 33; tarsus ♂ 13.

Range: Horne Islands (Futuna)

Halcyon chloris manuae Mayr, 1941

1941   *Halcyon chloris manuae* Mayr, Amer. Mus. Novit., 1152:2 (Manua Islands, Samoa, Tau)

Description: Differs from *H. c. sacra* by having the upperparts greener, loral spot larger, white collar wider, and nuchal collar darker. Males have loral spot and white collar washed with ochre. Wing ♂ 98, ♀ 100.

Range: American Samoa (Ofu, Olosega, Tau)

Halcyon chloris pealei Finsch and Hartlaub, 1868

1848   *Halcyon coronata* Peale, U. S. Expl. Expd., **8**:160 (Tutuila)
1868   *Halcyon Pealei* Finsch and Hartlaub, Beitr. Fauna Cent., Orn., p. 38 (Tutuila, Samoa) (new name for *Halcyon coronata* Peale; not *H. coronata* S. Müller, 1843)
1892   *Halcyon tutuilae* Sharpe, Cat. Bds. Brit. Mus., **17**:266 (Tutuila, Samoan Islands)

Description: Differs from *H. c. manuae* by having the forehead white, washed with rufous in the males, and the white collar wider. Wing ♂ 96, ♀ 99.
Range: American Samoa (Tutuila)

Remarks: This kingfisher is a common bird found throughout the islands from the seacoast to the forest streams. It is most often seen sitting on a dead limb or telephone wire.

SOCIETY ISLANDS KINGFISHER   PLATE 21

Halcyon venerata venerata (Gmelin, 1788)

1788   *Alcedo venerata* Gmelin, Syst. Nat., **1**:453 (Insula amici = Society Islands)
1848   *Dacelo nullitorquis* Peale, U. S. Expl. Expd., **8**:155 (Tahiti)

Description: Upperparts brownish green, crown paler, primaries and rectrices greener; nasal tufts dirty white; indistinct superciliary and ear-coverts greenish; underparts white, breast mottled with black streaks. Immature—upperparts browner and with a dark brown breast band.
Soft Parts: Bill, upper mandible black, lower mandible black with a white base; iris brown; feet purplish black.
Measurements: Wing ♂ 102, ♀ 108; tail 76; bill 39; tarsus 18.
Range: Society Islands (Tahiti)

Halcyon venerata youngi (Sharpe, 1892)

1892   *Todirhamphus youngi* Sharpe, Cat. Bds. Brit. Mus., **17**:289 ("Morea" = Moorea, Society Islands)

Description: Differs from *H. v. venerata* by having the upperparts brown, feathers edged with white; nasal tuft larger; ear-coverts brown, lacking the green. Underparts similar.
Range: Society Islands (Moorea)

Remarks: A common bird of the original forest near stream beds, this bird is most often heard calling during the early hours of the day.

SOUTH PACIFIC KINGFISHER   PLATE 21

Halcyon tuta tuta (Gmelin, 1788)

1788   *Alcedo tuta* Gmelin, Syst. Nat., **1**:423 (Tahiti)
1906   *Todirhamphus wiglesworthi* Sharpe, Hist. Coll. Brit. Mus., Bds., p. 182 (Society Islands)

Description: Male—crown green followed by a black band on hind neck; forehead, eyebrow stripe, and collar white; rest of upperparts dark blue-green; ear-coverts blue-green; underparts pure white. Female —similar to male but blue-green areas paler.
Soft Parts: Bill, upper mandible black, lower mandible black with a white base; iris brown; feet black.
Measurements: Wing ♂ 102, ♀ 104; tail 79; bill 39; tarsus 16.
Range: Society Islands (Bora-Bora, Huahine, Raiatea, Tahiti)

Halcyon tuta ruficollaris Holyoak, 1974

1974   *Halcyon ruficollaris* Holyoak, Bull. Brit. Orn. Cl., **94**:147 (Mangaia, Cook Islands)

Description: Differs from *H. t. tuta* by having the forehead, stripe over eye, nape, and upper breast orange-buff.
Range: Cook Islands (Mangaia)

Halcyon tuta atiu Holyoak, 1974

1974   *Halcyon tuta atiu* Holyoak, Bull. Brit. Orn. Cl., **94**:148 (Atiu, Cook Islands)

Description: Differs from *H. t. tuta* by having the white on the crown much more extensive—only a small blue-green remains in the center of the crown.
Range: Cook Islands (Atiu)

Halcyon tuta mauke Holyoak, 1974

1974   *Halcyon tuta mauke* Holyoak, Bull. Brit. Orn. Cl., **94**:148 (Mauke, Cook Islands)

Description: Differs from *H. t. atiu* by having the white of the crown reduced much like *H. t. tuta;* the feathers of the forehead, face, breast, and belly with a light buffy wash. This race is very weak, almost interme- diate between *H. t. ruficollaris* and *H. t. atiu* but much closer to *H. t. atiu.*
Range: Cook Islands (Mauke)

Remarks: A bird of the stream beds in the original forest, it is often seen sitting on palm fronds and dead stubs.

TUAMOTU KINGFISHER   PLATE 21

Halcyon gertrudae (Murphy, 1924)

1924   *Todirhamphus gertrudae* Murphy, Am. Mus. Novit., 149:1 (Niau, Tuamotu Archipelago)

Description: Crown, ear-coverts, collar on hind neck, back, wings, and tail blue-green; scapulars and rump brighter; forehead, lores, stripe over eye, and collar buffy white; underparts white, some individuals having a trace of a buffy breast band.

Soft Parts: Bill, upper mandible black, lower mandible black with a whitish base; iris brown; feet black.

Measurements: Wing ♂ 89, ♀ 93; tail 67; bill 37; tarsus 16.

Range: Tuamotu Archipelago (Niau)*

Remarks: Although usually found sitting in coconut trees, this bird may also be found in local towns.

MARQUESAS KINGFISHER   PLATE 21

Halcyon godeffroyi Finsch, 1877

1877   *Halcyon godeffroyi* Finsch, Proc. Zool. Soc. London, p. 408 (Marquesas Islands)

Description: Forehead, crown, mantle, and center of upper back white; lower back, rump, tail, and wings blue-green; lores, ear-coverts, and collar on hind neck black washed with green; underparts pure white. Immature has green crown.

Soft Parts: Bill, upper mandible black, lower mandible black with a white base; iris brown; feet black.

Measurements: Wing ♂ 97, ♀ 98; tail 75; bill 43; tarsus 14.

Range: Marquesas Islands (Hiva Oa, Tahuata)

Remarks: This kingfisher is a forest bird, usually found along streams in original forest. Its loud call can be heard for some distance.

---

*1895 *Halcyon gambieri* Oustalet, Nouv. Arch. Mus. Hist. Nat. Paris, **7**:182 (Mangareva, Tuamotu Archipelago). This doubtful species has been found only once, and the Mangareva type locality is questionable. At this time it is speculated that the specimen may have come from Micronesia.

PACIFIC SWALLOW PLATE 22

Hirundo tahitica subfusca Gould, 1856

1856 *Hirundo subfusca* Gould, Proc. Zool. Soc. London, p. 24 (Moala, Fiji)

Description: Forehead dark chestnut; top of head, back, and rump glossy steel-blue; wings and tail dull brownish black; chin and throat chestnut; breast and belly dark gray-brown with a few glossy, blackish brown feathers in the center of the breast.

Soft Parts: Bill black; iris brown; feet black.

Measurements: Wing ♂ 112, ♀ 99; tail ♂ 52, ♀ 48; bill 10; tarsus 11.

Range: Fiji (Komo, Lakemba, Mango, Matathawa Levu, Moala, Mothe, Naitaumba, Naviti, Nayau, Nggamea, Onega Levu, Taveuni, Thithia, Totoya, Viti Levu, Vomo)
Tonga (Kelefesia, Nomuka)

Hirundo tahitica tahitica Gmelin, 1789

1789 *Hirundo tahitica* Gmelin, Syst. Nat., **1**:1016 (Tahiti)

Description: Differs from *H. t. subfusca* by having the dark chestnut forehead reduced and much darker and the chin and throat paler chestnut; rest of underparts brownish black.

Range: Society Islands (Moorea, Tahiti)

Remarks: This swallow is found throughout the islands.

POLYNESIAN TRILLER PLATE 22

Lalage maculosa maculosa (Peale, 1848)

1848 *Colluricincla maculosa* Peale, U. S. Expl. Expd., **8**:81 (Upolu Island, Samoa)

Description: Male—upperparts glossy black; rump gray barred with black; wings black with white wing-coverts; tail black, rectrices tipped with white; lores and superciliary stripe white, a black stripe through the eye; underparts white. Female—similar to male but upperparts tend to be more blackish brown. Immature—blackish brown above, the crown with paler streaks; underparts with narrow black bars.

Soft Parts: Bill black; iris dark brown; feet dark blue-gray.

Measurements: Wing ♂ 96, ♀ 95; tail ♂ 67, ♀ 66; bill 16; tarsus 25.

Range: Western Samoa (Savaii, Upolu)

Lalage maculosa whitmeei Sharpe, 1878

1878   *Lalage whitmeei* Sharpe, Mitt. Zool. Mus. Dresden, **1**:371 (Savage Island)

Description: Differs from *L. m. maculosa* by having the rump darker, feathers tipped with black not gray-white, and superciliary stripe broader.

Range: Niue

Lalage maculosa futunae Mayr and Ripley, 1941

1941   *Lalage maculosa futunae* Mayr and Ripley, Am. Mus. Novit., 1116:6 (Futuna Island)

Description: Differs from *L. m. maculosa* by having the rump darker, the white on the wing-coverts more extensive, and a slightly shorter wing (♂ 92.5).

Range: Horne Islands (Futuna)

Lalage maculosa keppeli Mayr and Ripley, 1941

1941   *Lalage maculosa keppeli* Mayr and Ripley, Am. Mus. Novit., 1116:6 (Keppel I.)

Description: Differs from *L. m. maculosa* by having the feathers of the back and rump tipped with white, an indistinct white nuchal collar, the white tips on the rectrices more extensive, and the wing longer (♂ 99, ♀ 98). Tail ♂ 69, ♀ 68.

Range: Tonga (Niuatoputapu, Tafahi)

Lalage maculosa vauana Mayr and Ripley, 1941

1941   *Lalage maculosa vauana* Mayr and Ripley, Am. Mus. Novit., 1116:7 (Vavau I., Tonga Is.)

Description: Differs from *L. m. maculosa* by having the rump paler gray, the gray extending up onto the lower back; the wing-coverts more extensively marked with white; and the outer margins of the secondaries white.

Range: Tonga (Euakafa, Kapa, Late, Ovaka, Vavau)

Lalage maculosa tabuensis Mayr and Ripley, 1941

1941   *Lalage maculosa tabuensis* Mayr and Ripley, Am. Mus. Novit., 1116:7 (Tongatabu I., Tonga Is.)

Description: Differs from *L. m. vauana* by having the back feathers with white edges and a distinguishable nuchal collar.
Range: Tonga (Eua, Foa, Fotuhaa, Haafeva, Kao, Kelefesia, Lifuka, Mango, Nomuka, Oua, Telekitonga, Tofua, Tongatapu, Tonumea, Tungua, Uoleva, Uonuku Hahake)

Lalage maculosa nesophila Mayr and Ripley, 1941

1941 *Lalage maculosa nesophila* Mayr and Ripley, Am. Mus. Novit., 1116:8 (Ongea Levu I., Fiji Is.)

Description: Differs from *L. m. keppeli* by having the back feathers with narrower white tips and a whiter rump.
Range: Fiji (Aiwa, Fulanga, Kambara, Lakemba, Marambo, Matuku, Mothe, Namuka -I-Lau, Olorua, Oneata, Ongea Levu, Ono-I-Lau, Tavunasithi, Vatoa, Vatuvara, Wanggava, Yangasalevu, Yathata)

Lalage maculosa woodi Wetmore, 1925

1925 *Lalage woodi* Wetmore, Ibis, p. 845 (Taveuni, Fiji)

Description: Differs from *L. m. maculosa* by having the upperparts lightly washed with brown; white in wing-coverts reduced; sides of face, neck, and breast barred with brownish black; also, shorter wing (♂ 90, ♀ 88). Tail ♂ 61, ♀ 59.
Range: Fiji (Kio, Nggamea, Taveuni, Vanua Levu)

Lalage maculosa rotumae Neumann, 1927

1927 *Lalage nigra rotumae* Neumann, Orn. Monatsb., **35**:19 (Rotuma I.)

Description: Differs from *L. m. woodi* by having the white tips of the feathers of the back, rump, and wing-coverts washed with buff and the underparts, especially the breast, lightly washed with bright tawny; also, longer wing (♂ 94, ♀ 94). Tail ♂ 68, ♀ 65.
Range: Rotuma

Lalage maculosa mixta Mayr and Ripley, 1941

1941 *Lalage maculosa mixta* Mayr and Ripley, Am. Mus. Novit., 1116:9 (Ovalau I.)

Description: Differs from *L. m. woodi* by having the rusty brownish black upperparts washed with buff; gray rump washed with a reddish buff; underparts washed with buff; also, shorter wing (♂ 86, ♀ 85). Tail ♂ 61, ♀ 60.
Range: Fiji (Matathawa Levu, Mathuata, Naviti, Ovalau, Yandua, Yasawa)

PLATE 21

PLATE 21

SANDSTRÖM

PLATE 22

A WHITE-RUMPED SWIFTLET
   (*Collocalia spodiopygia spodiopygia*), male—page 101

B TAHITI SWIFTLET
   (*Collocalia leucophaea leucophaea*), male—page 106

C PACIFIC SWALLOW
   (*Hirundo tahitica subfusca*), male—page 113

D POLYNESIAN TRILLER
   (*Lalage maculosa maculosa*), male—page 113

E POLYNESIAN TRILLER
   (*Lalage maculosa rotumae*), male—page 115

F POLYNESIAN TRILLER
   (*Lalage maculosa pumila*), male—page 120

G SAMOAN TRILLER
   (*Lalage sharpei sharpei*), male—page 120

H RED-VENTED BULBUL
   (*Pycnonotus cafer bengalensis*), male—page 121

PLATE 22

Lalage maculosa pumila Neumann, 1927

1927   *Lalage nigra pumila* Neumann, Orn. Monatsb., **35**:19 (Viti Levu, Fiji Is.)

Description: Differs from *L. m. woodi* by having the upperparts brownish black; underparts more heavily washed with buff; and the barring of the sides of face, throat, and breast heavier and more extensive.
Range: Fiji (Viti Levu)

Lalage maculosa soror Mayr and Ripley, 1941

1941   *Lalage maculosa soror* Mayr and Ripley, Am. Mus. Novit., 1116:10 (Kandavu I.)

Description: Differs from *L. m. pumila* by having the top of the head black, contrasting with the blackish brown back; rump more clearly gray; underparts with less buffy wash and reduced barring.
Range: Fiji (Kandavu)

Remarks: A common bird, it may be found from sea level to the mountain tops.

SAMOAN TRILLER   PLATE 22

Lalage sharpei sharpei Rothschild, 1900

1900   *Lalage sharpei* Rothschild, Bull. Brit. Orn. Cl., **10**:40 (Upolu I., Samoa)

Description: Upperparts pale brown; underparts white with the chest and flanks lightly barred with brown.
Soft Parts: Bill yellow; iris white; feet brown.
Measurements: Wing ♂ 82, ♀ 81; tail ♂ 56, ♀ 55; bill 16; tarsus 23.
Range: Western Samoa (Upolu)

Lalage sharpei tenebrosa Mayr and Ripley, 1941

1941   *Lalage sharpei tenebrosa* Mayr and Ripley, Am. Mus. Novit., 1116:12 (Savaii I., Samoa)

Description: Differs from *L. s. sharpei* by having the upperparts darker and more olive-brown and the barring of the underparts darker and heavier.
Range: Western Samoa (Savaii)

Remarks: Usually found above 2000 feet in dense forest, this bird likes to sit on the dead limbs of large trees about 50 feet off the ground. It is very shy.

RED-VENTED BULBUL   PLATE 22

Pycnonotus cafer bengalensis Blyth, 1845

1845   *P(ycnonotus) bengalensis* Blyth, Journ. As. Soc. Bengal, **14**:566 (Bengal)

Description: Top of head black; back and wings dark brown; rump white; tail dark brown and rectrices tipped with white; ear-coverts brown; chin, throat, and upper breast blackish brown; belly gray-brown; vent and under tail-coverts bright red.

Soft Parts: Bill black; iris dark brown; feet black.

Measurements: Wing ♂ 108, ♀ 106; tail ♂ 101, ♀ 100; bill 18; tarsus 23.

Range: Introduced from India to American Samoa (Tutuila), Fiji (Le-
          leuvia, Nukulau, Viti Levu), and Western Samoa (Savaii,
          Upolu).

Remarks: This bird is common in lowlands and up to 3000 feet in the mountains.

ISLAND THRUSH   PLATE 23

Turdus poliocephalus*

This thrush is widespread on islands in the Pacific, with six of a total of 50 subspecies being found in the South Pacific. These shy birds are usually found above 1500 feet in dense mountain forests, where they dart through the thick cover near the forest floor. All six races are quite distinct.

Turdus ulietensis Gmelin, 1789, Syst. Nat., **1**:815 (Ulieta = Raiatea, Society Islands); *Turdus badius* Forster, 1844, Descr. Anim., p. 239 (Oriadea insula = Raiatea, Society Islands). This rufous-brown thrush-sized bird is known only from drawings; specimens collected during the eighteenth century have been lost and this species is presumed extinct. There is no assurance that it was really a *Turdus* or even a true thrush.

Turdus poliocephalus samoensis Tristram, 1879

1879   *Turdus samoensis* Tristram, Ibis, p. 188 (Samoa Islands)

Description: Entire bird dull black except for head and throat, which are very dark black-brown. Immature—underparts slightly spotted.
Soft Parts: Bill yellow; iris brown; feet yellow.
Measurements: Wing ♂ 100, ♀ 97; tail ♂ 77, ♀ 76; bill 22; tarsus 30.
Range: Western Samoa (Savaii, Upolu)

Turdus poliocephalus ruficeps (Ramsay, 1876)

1876   *Merula ruficeps* Ramsay, (Feb.) Proc. Linn. Soc. New South Wales, 1:43 (Fiji Islands = Kandavu)
1876   *Merula bicolor* Layard, (April) Ibis, p. 153 (Fiji)

Description: Head, hind neck, chin, and throat golden buff; rest of bird black. Immature—similar to adults but underparts rufous with black spots.
Soft Parts: Bill yellow; iris brown; feet yellow.
Measurements: Wing ♂ 106, ♀ 105; tail ♂ 71, ♀ 69; bill 24; tarsus 33.
Range: Fiji (Kandavu)

Turdus poliocephalus layardi (Seebohm, 1890)

1890   *Merula layardi* Seebohm, Proc. Zool. Soc. London, p. 667 (Viti Levu)

Description: Upperparts olive-gray; chin and throat gray-brown; breast and flanks chestnut; center of belly whitish. Immature—underparts paler and spotted.
Soft Parts: Bill yellow; iris brown; feet yellow.
Measurements: Wing ♂ 108, ♀ 107; tail ♂ 78, ♀ 78; bill 24; tarsus 34.
Range: Fiji (Koro, Ovalau, Viti Levu, Yasawa)

Turdus poliocephalus vitiensis Layard, 1876

1876   *Turdus vitiensis* Layard, Ann. Mag. Nat. Hist., Ser. 4, No. 17, p. 305 (Bua, Vanua Levu, Fiji)
1890   *Merula vanuensis* Seebohm, Proc. Zool. Soc. London, p. 666 (*nom. nov.* for *Merula vitiensis* Layard, 1876)

Description: Male—upperparts blackish gray; underparts gray. Female—similar to male but breast and belly washed with chestnut. Immature—underparts paler and spotted.
Soft Parts: Bill yellow; iris brown; feet yellow.
Measurements: Wing ♂ 111, ♀ 106; tail ♂ 77, ♀ 75; bill 24; tarsus 33.
Range: Fiji (Vanua Levu)

Turdus poliocephalus tempesti Layard, 1876

1876   *Turdus tempesti* Layard, Proc. Zool. Soc. London, p. 420 (south end of Taveuni, at Selia Levu, Vuna Point)

Description: Male—head, hind neck, chin, and throat gray; rest of bird black. Female—differs from male by having gray areas dark brown. Immature—underparts paler and spotted.
Soft Parts: Bill yellow; iris yellow; feet yellow.
Measurements: Wing ♂ 109, ♀ 105; tail ♂ 78, ♀ 71; bill 25; tarsus 33.
Range: Fiji (Taveuni)

Turdus poliocephalus hades Mayr, 1941

1941   *Turdus poliocephalus hades* Mayr, Am. Mus. Novit., 1152:4 (Ngau Island, Fiji)

Description: Entire male black, the darkest of all the South Pacific races. Female undescribed. Immature male with reddish brown edgings on underparts.
Soft Parts: Bill yellow; iris brown; feet yellow.
Measurements: Wing ♂ 110; tail ♂ 75; bill ♂ 24; tarsus ♂ 33.
Range: Fiji (Ngau)

LONG-BILLED WARBLER   PLATE 24

Conopoderas caffra caffra (Sparrman, 1786)

1786   *Sitta caffra* Sparrman, Mus. Carls., fasc. I, pl. 4 (no locality = Tahiti)
1842   *Tatare fuscus* Lesson, Rev. Zool., **5**:210 (Tahiti)

Description: Upperparts olive-brown mottled with yellow; superciliary stripe and underparts white washed with yellow. Immature—darker brown.
Soft Parts: Bill, upper mandible black, lower mandible flesh color; iris brown; feet grayish.
Measurements: Wing ♂ 97, ♀ 93; tail ♂ 78, ♀ 74; bill 26; tarsus 30.
Range: Society Islands (Tahiti)

Conopoderas caffra longirostris (Gmelin, 1789)

1789   *Turdus longirostris* Gmelin, Syst. Nat., **1**:823 (Eimeo = Moorea, Society Islands)

Description: Differs from *C. c. caffra* by being larger (wing ♂ 105, ♀ 103; tail ♂ 89, ♀ 85; bill 29).
Range: Society Islands (Moorea)

Conopoderas caffra percernis Wetmore, 1919

1919   *Conopoderas percernis* Wetmore, Bull. Mus. Comp. Zool., **63**:213 (Nukuhiva, Marquesas)

Description: Differs from *C. c. caffra* by having the yellows richer, longer wing (♂ 100, ♀ 98), longer tail (♂ 85, ♀ 82), and shorter bill (23).
Range: Marquesas Islands (Nuku Hiva)

Conopoderas caffra mendanae (Tristram, 1883)

1883   *Acrocephalus mendanae* Tristram, Ibis, p. 43 (Marquesas Islands = Hivaoa, or Tahuata, Islands, Marquesas; restricted to Hivaoa by Murphy and Mathews)

Description: Differs from *C. c. percernis* by being paler, the yellows not as rich. Wing ♂ 99, ♀ 97; tail ♂ 82, ♀ 79; bill 24.
Range: Marquesas Islands (Hiva Oa, Tahuata)

Conopoderas caffra consobrina Murphy and Mathews, 1928

1928   *Conopoderas caffra consobrina* Murphy and Mathews, Am. Mus. Novit., 337:13 Motane Island, Marquesas)

Description: Differs from *C. c. mendanae* by having wider yellowish margins to the feathers of the upperparts; underparts with a heavier yellowish wash; also smaller (wing ♂ 96, ♀ 95; tail ♂ 80, ♀ 80; bill 21).
Range: Marquesas Islands (Motane)

Conopoderas caffra fatuhivae Murphy and Mathews, 1928

1928   *Conopoderas caffra fatuhivae* Murphy and Mathews, Am. Mus. Novit., 337:14 (Fatuhiva Island, Marquesas)

Description: Differs from *C. c. percernis* by having the rump brighter yellow, a longer bill (25), and a longer tarsus (33).
Range: Marquesas Islands (Fatu Hiva)

Conopoderas caffra idae Murphy and Mathews, 1928

1928   *Conopoderas caffra idae* Murphy and Mathews, Am. Mus. Novit., 337:15 (Huahuna Island, Marquesas)

Description: Differs from *C. c. percernis* by being smaller (wing ♂ 89, ♀ 88; tail ♂ 77, ♀ 75; bill 19; tarsus 30).
Range: Marquesas Islands (Ua Huna)

Conopoderas caffra dido Murphy and Mathews, 1928

1928   *Conopoderas caffra dido* Murphy and Mathews, Am. Mus. Novit., 337:16 (Huapu Island, Marquesas)

Description: Differs from *C. c. percernis* by having the underparts a brighter yellow; this is the brightest race of *C. caffra*. Also smaller (wing ♂ 93, ♀ 91; tail ♂ 79, ♀ 76; bill 21).
Range: Marquesas Islands (Ua Pu)

Conopoderas caffra aquilonis Murphy and Mathews, 1928

1928 *Conopoderas caffra aquilonis* Murphy and Mathews, Am. Mus. Novit., 337:17 (Eiao Island, Marquesas)

Description: Differs from *C. c. dido* by having the underparts slightly paler yellow and a smaller bill (19).
Range: Marquesas Islands (Eiao)

Conopoderas caffra postrema Murphy and Mathews, 1928

1928 *Conopoderas caffra postrema* Murphy and Mathews, Am. Mus. Novit., 337:17 (Hatutu Island, Marquesas)

Description: Differs from *C. c. aquilonis* by having the upperparts more olivaceous.
Range: Marquesas Islands (Hatutu)

Remarks: A bird of thick bush in mountain ravines, it is usually very shy but quite vocal. Its camouflaged color makes it very difficult to find. One specimen collected on Huahine in 1877 has been lost and its subspecific identity is unknown.

TUAMOTU WARBLER   PLATE 24

Conopoderas atypha atypha Wetmore, 1919

1919 *Conopoderas atypha* Wetmore, Bull. Mus. Comp. Zool., **63**:206 (Fakarava, Tuamotu Group)

1919 *Conopoderas atypha crypta* Wetmore, Bull. Mus. Comp. Zool., **63**:209 (Makemo, Tuamotu Group)

1919 *Conopoderas atypha agassizi* Wetmore, Bull. Mus. Comp. Zool., **63**:210 (Apataki, Tuamotu Group)

1919 *Conopoderas atypha nesiarcha* Wetmore, Bull. Mus. Comp. Zool., **63**:210 (Rangiroa, Tuamotu Group)

Description: Upperparts generally gray-brown, feathers often with fine, dirty white margins; wings and tail slightly darker gray-brown but tipped with white; superciliary stripe and underparts whitish. A highly variable species, tending toward grayish and brownish color phases.
Soft Parts: Bill, upper mandible black, lower mandible flesh color; iris brown; feet gray.
Measurements: Wing ♂ 88, ♀ 84; tail ♂ 74, ♀ 71; bill 21; tarsus 30.

Range: Tuamotu Archipelago (Ahe, Apataki, Aratika, Arutua, Faaite, Fakahina, Fakarava, Hiti, Katiu, Kauehi, Kaukura, Makemo, Manihi, Matahiva, Nihiru, Rangiroa, Raraka, Taenga, Tahanea, Taiaro, Takapoto, Takaroa, Takume, Tepoto, Tikehau, Tikei, Toau, Tuanake)

Conopoderas atypha palmarum Murphy and Mathews, 1929

1929   *Conopoderas atypha palmarum* Murphy and Mathews, Am. Mus. Novit., 350:12 (Anaa Island, Tuamotus)

Description: Differs from *C. a. atypha* by being smaller (wing ♂ 86, ♀ 80; tail ♂ 71, ♀ 63; bill 18).
Range: Tuamotu Archipelago (Anaa)

Conopoderas atypha niauensis Murphy and Mathews, 1929

1929   *Conopoderas atypha niauensis* Murphy and Mathews, Am. Mus. Novit., 350:13 (Niau Island, Tuamotus)

Description: Differs from *C. a. atypha* by almost lacking the superciliary stripe and the white feather margins of the back and by being smaller (wing ♂ 85, ♀ 79; tail ♂ 71, ♀ 65; bill 18).
Range: Tuamotu Archipelago (Niau)

Conopoderas atypha rava Wetmore, 1919

1919   *Conopoderas atypha rava* Wetmore, Bull. Mus. Comp. Zool., **63**:208 (Pinaki or Whitsunday Island, Tuamotus)

Description: Differs from *C. a. atypha* by having the underparts washed with yellow.
Range: Tuamotu Archipelago (Akiaki, Fagataufa, Hao, Paraoa, Pinaki, Tureia, Vanavana)

Conopoderas atypha erema Wetmore, 1919

1919   *Conopoderas atypha erema* Wetmore, Bull. Mus. Comp. Zool., **63**:211 (Makatea, Tuamotus)

Description: Differs from *C. a. atypha* by being entirely washed with cinnamon; also larger (wing ♂ 92, ♀ 89; tail ♂ 80, ♀ 76; bill 24 and markedly decurved).
Range: Tuamotu Archipelago (Makatea)

Conopoderas atypha flavida Murphy and Mathews, 1929

1929   *Conopoderas atypha flavida* Murphy and Mathews, Am. Mus. Novit., 350:16 (Napuka Island, Tuamotus)

Description: Differs from *C. a. atypha* by having the upperparts slightly and the underparts strongly washed with yellow; also larger (wing ♂ 93, tail ♂ 75, bill ♂ 24, tarsus ♂ 31; female unknown).
Range: Tuamotu Archipelago (Napuka)

Remarks: A bird of open, brushy country and woodland, it is often seen sitting on high branches of trees giving its very loud and variable call.

PITCAIRN ISLAND REED-WARBLER   PLATE 24

Conopoderas vaughani vaughani (Sharpe, 1900)

1900 *Tatare vaughani* Sharpe, Bull. Brit. Orn. Cl., **11**:2 (Pitcairn Island)

Description: Upperparts olive, margins of feathers buffy; wing dark olive-brown with some albinistic feathers; tail olive-brown, rectrices tipped with white, some albinistic feathers; underparts yellowish with a buffy wash on flanks. Immature—differs by being browner above and seems to lack albinistic feathers.
Soft Parts: Bill, upper mandible blackish brown, lower mandible flesh color; iris brown; feet grayish.
Measurements: Wing ♂ 82, ♀ 75; tail ♂ 70, ♀ 65; bill 17; tarsus 29.
Range: Pitcairn Island

Conopoderas vaughani rimitarae Murphy and Mathews, 1929

1929 *Conopoderas vaughani rimitarae* Murphy and Mathews, Am. Mus. Novit.,
        350:20 (Rimitara Island, Austral Group)

Description: Differs from *C. v. vaughani* by having the upperparts darker olive; also larger (wing ♂ 84, ♀ 82; tail ♂ 71, ♀ 71). Albinism more noticeable.
Range: Austral Islands (Rimatara)

Conopoderas vaughani taiti (Ogilvie-Grant, 1913)

1913 *Acrocephalus taiti* Ogilvie-Grant, Bull. Brit. Orn. Cl., **31**:59 (Henderson
        Island)

Description: Differs from *C. v. vaughani* by lacking olive and yellow tints, being basically brown above and white below. Albinistic feathers found throughout the body and to a greater extent than in *C. v. rimitarae*.
Range: Henderson Island

Conopoderas vaughani kerearako (Holyoak, 1974)

1974   *Acrocephalus vaughani kerearako* Holyoak, Bull. Brit. Orn. Cl., **94**:149 (Mangaia, Cook Islands)

Description: Differs from *C. v. rimitarae* by having the upperparts more olive and the underparts yellower.

Range: Cook Islands (Mangaia)

Conopoderas vaughani kaoko (Holyoak, 1974)

1974   *Acrocephalus vaughani kaoko* Holyoak, Bull. Brit. Orn. Cl., **94**:150 (Mitiaro, Cook Islands)

Description: Differs from *C. v. kerearako* by having the upperparts duller olive-brown; underparts paler yellow and slightly streaked with gray on the throat and breast; thighs light brown.

Range: Cook Islands (Mitiaro)

Remarks: The habits of this bird are unknown.

LONG-LEGGED WARBLER   PLATE 24

Trichocichla rufa Reichenow, 1890

1890   *Trichocichla rufa* Reichenow, Journ. f. Orn., **38**:489 (Viti Levu, Fiji)

Description: Upperparts rufous, the crown somewhat darker and the lower back and rump brighter; lores and stripe behind eye white becoming washed with rufous toward nape; chin and throat white; center of breast and belly whitish; rest of underparts rufous.

Soft Parts: Bill in dried specimen dark brown above, horn colored below; iris brown; feet pinkish.

Measurements: One specimen—wing ♂ 78, tail ♂ 81, bill ♂ 20, tarsus ♂ 29.

Range: Fiji (Viti Levu)

Remarks: Known from only a few specimens and records during the last century, this bird has recently been rediscovered on Vanua Levu by Kinsky from the National Museum of New Zealand (1975, Bull. Brit. Orn. Cl., **95**:98-101). It lives in dense rain forest.

FIJI WARBLER PLATE 24

Vitia ruficapilla ruficapilla Ramsay, 1876

1876   *Vitia ruficapilla* Ramsay, Proc. Linn. Soc. New South Wales, **1**:41 (Kandavu, Fiji)

Description: Top of head and cheeks bright rufous, rest of upperparts grayish olive-brown; chin, throat, breast, and belly grayish white; flanks brownish. Immature—underparts browner.

Soft Parts: Bill, upper mandible brown, lower mandible horn; iris brown; feet flesh color.

Measurements: Wing ♂ 59, ♀ 53; tail ♂ 58, ♀ 46; bill 15; tarsus 24.

Range: Fiji (Kandavu)

Vitia ruficapilla badiceps (Finsch, 1876)

1876   *Drymochaera badiceps* Finsch, Proc. Zool. Soc. London, p. 20 (Viti Levu, Fiji)

Description: Differs from *V. r. ruficapilla* by having the bright rufous on the head reduced to the crown; cheeks gray; a dark line through the eye; also, shorter wing (♂ 54, ♀ 52).

Range: Fiji (Viti Levu)

Vitia ruficapilla castaneoptera Mayr, 1935

1935   *Vitia ruficapilla castaneoptera* Mayr, Am. Mus. Novit., 820:5 (Vanua Levu, Fiji)

Description: Differs from *V. r. badiceps* by having the wings and tail browner; size as in *V. r. ruficapilla* (wing ♂ 59).

Range: Fiji (Vanua Levu)

Vitia ruficapilla funebris Mayr, 1935

1935   *Vitia ruficapilla funebris* Mayr, Am. Mus. Novit., 820:5 (Taviuni, Fiji)

Description: Differs from *V. r. badiceps* by being darker, having chestnut cheeks, and being larger (wing ♂ 62).

Range: Fiji (Taveuni)

Remarks: This warbler is a bird of low bushes in the upland forest; its seclusiveness makes it difficult to find.

130

PLATE 23

A   ISLAND THRUSH
(*Turdus poliocephalus ruficeps*), male—page 122

B   ISLAND THRUSH
(*Turdus poliocephalus samoensis*), male—page 122

C   ISLAND THRUSH
(*Turdus poliocephalus vitiensis*), male—page 122

D   ISLAND THRUSH
(*Turdus poliocephalus layardi*), male—page 122

E   ISLAND THRUSH
(*Turdus poliocephalus hades*), male—page 123

F   ISLAND THRUSH
(*Turdus poliocephalus tempesti*), male—page 122

A

B

C

D

E

F

SANDSTRÖM

PLATE 23

PLATE 24

SANDSTRÖM

PLATE 24

SILKTAIL   PLATE 24

Lamprolia victoriae victoriae Finsch, 1873

1873   *Lamprolia victoriae* Finsch, Proc. Zool. Soc. London, p. 735 (Taviuni, Fiji)

Description: Entire bird velvet-black except for feathers on top of head, chin, and throat, which have metallic blue spangles; rump white; central rectrices white with black tips glossed with metallic blue-black.
Soft Parts: Bill black; iris brown; feet black.
Measurements: Wing ♂ 84, ♀ 82; tail ♂ 53, ♀ 50; bill 13; tarsus 23.
Range: Fiji (Taveuni)

Lamprolia victoriae kleinschmidti Ramsay, 1876

1876   *Lamprolia kleinschmidti* Ramsay, Proc. Linn. Soc. New South Wales, 1:68 (Vanua Levu)

1876   *Lamprolia minor* Layard, Ibis, p. 155 (Vanua Levu)

Description: Differs from *L. v. victoriae* by having the spangles on the head bluer. Also smaller (wing ♂ 76, ♀ 74; tail ♂ 49, ♀ 48).
Range: Fiji (Vanua Levu)

Remarks: A bird of the forest, it is found above 1500 feet, usually within 20 feet of the ground. This beautiful little bird is one of the most spectacular birds of the South Pacific.

SCARLET ROBIN   PLATE 24

Petroica multicolor pusilla Peale, 1848

1848   *Petroica pusilla* Peale, U. S. Expl. Expd., 8:93 (Upolu, Samoa)

Description: Male—forehead white, rest of upperparts black; primaries and rectrices brownish black, outer rectrices tipped with white; white patch in secondaries; wing bar white; chin and upper throat black; lower throat, breast, and belly pale vermilion; under tail-coverts white; thighs black. Female—similar to male; reduced white on forehead; chin and upper throat gray-black; vermilion of underparts paler and with a whitish patch in the center of the belly. Immature—similar to female but duller.
Soft Parts: Bill black; iris brown; feet brownish.
Measurements: Wing ♂ 61, ♀ 59; tail ♂ 38, ♀ 37; bill 11; tarsus 17.
Range: Western Samoa (Savaii, Upolu)

Petroica multicolor kleinschmidti Finsch, 1875

1875 *Petroica kleinschmidti* Finsch, Proc. Zool. Soc. London, p. 643 (Viti Levu, Fiji)

Description: Differs from *P. m. pusilla* by the male having the white patch on forehead larger, the back richer black, and the white wing bar more extensive. The female has blackish brown upperparts and the vermilion of the underparts is duller and less extensive, especially the belly, which is almost all whitish.
Range: Fiji (Taveuni, Vanua Levu, Viti Levu)

Petroica multicolor becki Mayr, 1934

1934 *Petroica multicolor becki* Mayr, Am. Mus. Novit., 714:5 (Kandavu, Fiji)

Description: Males differ from *P. m. kleinschmidti* by having the throat redder and the vermilion on the flanks more extensive. Females have browner upperparts.
Range: Fiji (Kandavu)

Remarks: This is a common bird of clearings and the forest edge.

RAROTONGA FLYCATCHER   PLATE 25

Pomarea dimidiata (Hartlaub and Finsch, 1871)

1871 *Monarches dimidiata* Hartlaub and Finsch, Proc. Zool. Soc. London, p. 28 (Rarotonga, Cook Islands)

Description: Male—upperparts gray, rump and tail darker; underparts white except for under tail-covert feathers, which are blackish with white tips. Female—upperparts bright rufous except for wing primaries and the terminal quarter of the tail, which are blackish brown; underparts pale rufous, becoming paler in the center of the belly.
Soft Parts: Bill plumbeous-blue; iris dark brown; feet dark plumbeous.
Measurements: Wing ♂ 81, ♀ 76; tail ♂ 65, ♀ 61; bill 15; tarsus 21.
Range: Cook Islands (Rarotonga)

Remarks: The habits of this bird are unknown.

SOCIETY ISLANDS FLYCATCHER   PLATE 25

Pomarea nigra (Sparrman, 1786)

1786   *Muscicapa nigra* Sparrman, Mus. Carls., fasc. I, pl. 23 (Tahiti)

1789   *Muscicapa lutea* Gmelin, Syst. Nat., **1**:944 (Tahiti)

1828   *Muscicapa pomarea* Lesson and Garnot, Voy. "Coquille," pl. 17 (Maupiti Island)

1829   *Muscicapa maupitiensis* Lesson and Garnot, Voy. "Coquille," p. 592 (Maupiti Island)

1844   *Muscicapa atra* Forster, Descr. Anim., ed. Licht., p. 170 (Tahiti)

1929   *Pomarea nigra tabuensis* Mathews, Bull. Brit. Orn. Cl., **49**:60 (new name for *Muscicapa atra* Forster, 1844, p. 171; not Forster 1844, p. 170)

Description: Adults entirely black. Immature—upperparts dark cinnamon except rump, which is black; underparts pale cinnamon, becoming almost white on the belly.

Soft Parts: Bill slaty blue; iris dark brown; feet slaty blue.

Measurements: Wing ♂ 89, ♀ 86; tail 74; bill 16; tarsus 27.

Range: Society Islands (Maupiti, Tahiti)

Remarks: This secretive bird lives in the fern-covered canyons of the mountain slopes.

MARQUESAS FLYCATCHER   PLATE 25

Pomarea mendozae mendozae (Hartlaub, 1854)

1854   *Monarcha Mendozae* Hartlaub, Journ. f. Orn., **2**:170 (St. Christina = Tahuata Island, Marquesas)

Description: Male—entire bird glossy black. Female—head black; back and rump white; primaries black, secondaries black with white margins; tail white with brownish subterminal spots; breast and belly buffy white. Immature—brownish.

Soft Parts: Bill bluish; iris brown; legs bluish; feet black.

Measurements: Wing ♂ 92, ♀ 91; tail 78; bill 17; tarsus 28.

Range: Marquesas Islands (Hiva Oa, Tahuata)

Pomarea mendozae motanensis Murphy and Mathews, 1928

1928   *Pomarea mendozae motanensis* Murphy and Mathews, Am. Mus. Novit., 337:4 (Motane Island, Marquesas)

Description: Differs from *P. m. mendozae* by having the subterminal spots on the rectrices of females much reduced; also larger (wing ♂ 96, ♀ 95; bill 19). Immatures paler.
Range: Marquesas Islands (Motane)

Pomarea mendozae mira Murphy and Mathews, 1928

1928   *Pomarea mendozae mira* Murphy and Mathews, Am. Mus. Novit., 337:4 (Huapu Island, Marquesas)

Description: Females differ from *P. m. motanensis* by having entire body black; tail white; wings white with terminal third of primaries and secondaries brownish black; also larger (wing ♂ 108, ♀ 103).
Range: Marquesas Islands (Ua Pu)

Pomarea mendozae nukuhivae Murphy and Mathews, 1928

1928   *Pomarea mendozae nukuhivae* Murphy and Mathews, Am. Mus. Novit., 337:5 (Nukuhiva Island, Marquesas)

Description: Female differs from *P. m. mira* by having mantle and belly white.
Range: Marquesas Islands (Nuku Hiva)

Remarks: This bird of the low forest needs study because little is known of its habits.

ALLIED FLYCATCHER   PLATE 25

Pomarea iphis iphis Murphy and Mathews, 1928

1928   *Pomarea iphis* Murphy and Mathews, Am. Mus. Novit., 337:6 (Huahuna Island, Marquesas)

Description: Male—glossy black except for primaries, secondaries, and rectrices, which are brownish black; breast and belly mottled with black and white; under tail-coverts white. Female—top of head dark brown, rest of upperparts brown; underparts buffy white with black bases of throat feathers showing through. Immature—similar to female.
Soft Parts: Bill black; iris brown; feet black.
Measurements: Wing ♂ 94, ♀ 88; tail ♂ 80, ♀ 75; bill 17; tarsus 27.
Range: Marquesas Islands (Ua Huka)

Pomarea iphis fluxa Murphy and Mathews, 1928

1928   *Pomarea iphis fluxa* Murphy and Mathews, Am. Mus. Novit., 337:7 (Eiao Island, Marquesas)

Description: Differs from *P. i. iphis* by having the black and white mottled areas of the male more extensive (including the back and wing-coverts) and the throat of the female heavily streaked with black. Also smaller (wing ♂ 85, ♀ 82; tail ♂ 77, ♀ 71).
Range: Marquesas Islands (Eiao)

Remarks: This is a shy bird of the original forest; its habits are virtually unknown.

LARGE FLYCATCHER   PLATE 25

Pomarea whitneyi Murphy and Mathews, 1928

1928   *Pomarea whitneyi* Murphy and Mathews, Am. Mus. Novit., 337:8 (Fatu-hiva Island, Marquesas)

Description: Both male and female black. Immature—upperparts cinnamon-brown; underparts whitish.
Soft Parts: Bill bluish horn; iris brown; legs blue-gray; feet black.
Measurements: Wing 113; tail 101; bill 21; tarsus 32.
Range: Marquesas Islands (Fatu Hiva)

Remarks: The habits of this bird of the forest are unknown.

MAYR'S FLYCATCHER   PLATE 26

Mayrornis versicolor Mayr, 1933

1933   *Mayrornis versicolor* Mayr, Am. Mus. Novit., 651:19 (Ongea Levu, eastern Fiji)

Description: Upperparts dark gray; tail brownish gray tipped with buff; underparts pinkish cinnamon; chin and upper throat somewhat paler.
Soft Parts: Bill blue-black; iris brown; feet grayish.
Measurements: Wing ♂ 69, ♀ 66; tail ♂ 60, ♀ 58; bill 14; tarsus 18.
Range: Fiji (Ongea Levu)

Remarks: This flycatcher is a bird of the brushy lowlands and forest edges.

CINEREOUS FLYCATCHER   PLATE 26

Mayrornis lessoni lessoni (G. R. Gray, 1846)

1846   *R.[hipidura] Lessoni* G. R. Gray, Gen. Birds, **1**:258 (Ovalau)
1848   *Monarcha cinereus* Peale, U. S. Expl. Expd., **8**:101 (near Bahr = Mba, Viti Levu, Fiji)

Description: Upperparts gray, rump paler; upper tail-coverts black tipped with white; tail black and rectrices tipped with white, outermost almost one-half white; wings dull black, secondaries tipped with white; forehead, lores, and superciliary stripe white; underparts gray-white, belly somewhat whiter.
Soft Parts: Bill bluish; iris brown; feet grayish.
Measurements: Wing ♂ 69, ♀ 65; tail ♂ 59, ♀ 56; bill 14; tarsus 17.
Range: Fiji (Kandavu, Kio, Leleuvia, Malake, Mbengga, Mbulia, Nggamea, Ono, Ovalau, Rambi, Taveuni, Vanua Kula, Vanua Levu, Viti Levu, Vuro, Yanganga, Yanutha, Yaukuve Levu)

Mayrornis lessoni orientalis Mayr, 1933

1933   *Mayrornis lessoni orientalis* Mayr, Am. Mus. Novit., 651:18 (Yangasa Cluster, eastern Fiji)

Description: Differs from *M. l. lessoni* by having the rump uniform in color with the back, lacking white tips to the upper tail-coverts and secondaries, and having sides of face darker; also larger (wing ♂ 75, ♀ 71; tail ♂ 67, ♀ 64; bill 17; tarsus 20).
Range: Fiji (Aiwa, Explorers Islands, Kambara, Mango, Marambo, Moala, Mothe, Naitaumba, Namuka-I-Lau, Oneata, Ongea Levu, Thithia, Vanuavatu, Vatuvara, Wanggava, Yangasa-levu)

Remarks: A bird of the rain forest, it is most commonly found from 5 to 50 feet; it is not a shy bird.

FIJI SHRIKEBILL   PLATE 26

Clytorhynchus vitiensis vitiensis (Hartlaub, 1866)

1866   *Myiolestes vitiensis* Hartlaub, Ibis, p. 173 (Ovalau)

Description: Crown and back brown, rest of upperparts more reddish brown; rectrices tipped with buffy white; lores, superciliary stripe, and face gray-brown; underparts dirty gray; flanks and under tail-coverts reddish brown.

Soft Parts: Bill black; iris brown; feet bluish gray.
Measurements: Wing ♂ 88, ♀ 85; tail ♂ 75, ♀ 74; bill 22; tarsus 21.
Range: Fiji (Koro, Makongai, Mbengga, Namenalala, Ngau, Ovalau, Viti Levu, Wakaya)

Clytorhynchus vitiensis compressirostris (Layard, 1876)

1876   *Myiolestes compressirostris* Layard, Ibis, p. 153 (Kandavu Island)

Description: Differs from *C. v. vitiensis* by having the upperparts lighter and the underparts less grayish, more buffy; also smaller but with a longer bill (wing ♂ 86, ♀ 83; tail ♂ 72, ♀ 71; bill 23).
Range: Fiji (Kandavu, Ono, Vanua Kula)

Clytorhynchus vitiensis buensis (Layard, 1876)

1876   *M.[yiolestes] buensis* Layard, Ibis, p. 145 (Mbua Bay, Vanua Levu, Fiji)

Description: Differs from *C. v. vitiensis* by having the upperparts paler and washed with olive, sides of face grayer, and underparts less grayish and washed with olive-buff; also slightly larger (wing ♂ 90, ♀ 88; tail ♂ 78, ♀ 76; bill 23).
Range: Fiji (Kio, Vanua Levu)

Clytorhynchus vitiensis layardi Mayr, 1933

1875   *Pachycephala macrorhyncha* Layard, Proc. Zool. Soc. London, p. 150 (Taviuni) (not *Pachycephala macrorhyncha* Strickland, 1849)

1933   *Clytorhynchus vitiensis layardi* Mayr, Am. Mus. Novit., 628:9 (Taviuni Island, Fiji)

Description: Differs from *C. v. buensis* by having the upperparts more rufous, face grayer, underparts washed with olive-buff; also larger (wing ♂ 92, ♀ 88; tail ♂ 79, ♀ 76; bill 24).
Range: Fiji (Taveuni)

Clytorhynchus vitiensis pontifex Mayr, 1933

1933   *Clytorhynchus vitiensis pontifex* Mayr, Am. Mus. Novit., 628:11 (Ngamia Island, Fiji)

Description: Differs from *C. v. buensis* by having the underparts purer gray, under tail-coverts lighter; also larger (wing ♂ 95, ♀ 90; tail ♂ 80, ♀ 78; bill 24).
Range: Fiji (Nggamea, Rambi)

Clytorhynchus vitiensis vatuana Mayr, 1933

1933   *Clytorhynchus vitiensis vatuana* Mayr, Am. Mus. Novit., 628:12 (Tuvutha Island)

Description: Differs from *C. v. pontifex* by having the underparts slightly washed with buff; also slightly larger. A weakly defined race.

Range: Fiji (Tuvutha, Vatuvara, Yathata)

Clytorhynchus vitiensis nesiotes (Wetmore, 1919)

1919 *Pinarolestes nesiotes* Wetmore, Bull. Mus. Comp. Zool., **63**:216 (Kambara, Lau Archipelago, Fiji)

Description: Differs from *C. v. pontifex* and *vatuana* by having the upperparts duller rufous and the underparts paler gray, especially the belly; also larger (wing ♂ 100, ♀ 99).

Range: Fiji (Aiwa, Fulanga, Kambara, Namuka-I-Lau, Oneata, Ongea Levu, Wanggava, Yangasalevu)

Clytorhynchus vitiensis heinei (Finsch and Hartlaub, 1869)

1869 *Myiolestes heinei* Finsch and Hartlaub, Proc. Zool. Soc. London, p. 546 (Tonga Islands)

Description: Differs from *C. v. nesiotes* by having the face darker gray-black, underparts uniformly paler gray, and white tips on rectrices larger; also smaller (wing ♂ 97, ♀ 92; bill 25).

Range: Tonga (Fotuhaa, Kelefesia, Mango, Nomuka Iki, Ofolanga, Teaupa, Telekiaapai, Telekitonga, Tofonga, Tonumea, Tungua, Uoleva, Uonuku Hahake, Uonuku Hihifo)

Clytorhynchus vitiensis wiglesworthi Mayr, 1933

1933 *Clytorhynchus vitiensis wiglesworthi* Mayr, Am. Mus. Novit., 628:14 (Rotumah Island)

Description: Differs from *C. v. layardi* by having the face darker, underparts more grayish, buffy white tips on rectrices smaller, and a shorter tail (♂ 77, ♀ 74).

Range: Rotuma

Clytorhynchus vitiensis fortunae (Layard, 1876)

1876 *M. [yiolestes] fortunae* Layard, Ibis, p. 145 (Fortuna Island)

Description: The palest and smallest of all races. Upperparts light brown; face gray; underparts gray, belly almost white.

Measurements: Wing ♂ 84, ♀ 82; tail ♂ 70, ♀ 68; bill 21.

Range: Horne Islands (Alofi, Futuna)

Clytorhynchus vitiensis powelli (Salvin, 1879)

1879 *Pinarolestes powelli* Salvin, Proc. Zool. Soc. London, p. 128 (Tutuila = Manua Islands, Samoa)

Description: Differs from the Fiji and Tonga forms by having the upperparts darker, face darker gray, and the underparts darker, especially the flanks, which contrast with the pale gray belly.
Measurements: Wing ♂ 91, ♀ 88; tail ♂ 75, ♀ 73; bill 23.
Range: American Samoa (Ofu, Olosega, Tau)

Clytorhynchus vitiensis keppeli Mayr, 1933

1933   *Clytorhynchus vitiensis keppeli* Mayr, Am. Mus. Novit., 628:16 (Keppel Island)

Description: The darkest form. Upperparts dark brown; buffy white tips on rectrices almost absent and the underparts uniform dark gray-brown.
Range: Tonga (Niuatoputapu, Tafahi)

Remarks: This is a bird of the wet, dark forest.

BLACK-THROATED SHRIKE-THRUSH   PLATE 26

Clytorhynchus nigrogularis nigrogularis (Layard, 1875)

1875   *Lalage nigrogularis* Layard, Proc. Zool. Soc. London, p. 149 (Levuka, Ovalau Island)
1876   *Myiolestes maxima* Layard, Ibis, p. 498 (Kandavu Island)

Description: Male—crown and nape grayish brown; rest of upperparts olive-brown; wings and tail brownish; forehead, lores, superciliary, chin, throat, and patch behind ear-coverts black with a posterior silver-gray border; ear-coverts silver-gray; rest of underparts gray-brown. Female —upperparts reddish brown; underparts gray-brown; flanks and under tail-coverts reddish brown. Immature—like female. Individual variation —adults vary from relatively brownish to grayish.
Soft Parts: Bill black, tip horn colored; iris brown; feet bluish gray.
Measurements: Wing ♂ 104, ♀ 102; tail ♂ 86, ♀ 82; bill 28; tarsus 25.
Range: Fiji (Kandavu, Ovalau, Taveuni, Vanua Levu, Viti Levu)

Remarks: This bird of the dense forest forages on the ground; it is usually very difficult to find.

VANIKORO BROADBILL   PLATE 27

Myiagra vanikorensis rufiventris Elliot, 1859

1859 *Myiagra rufiventris* Elliot, Ibis, p. 393 (Samoan or Navigator's Islands = Viti Levu, Fiji)

1867 *Myiagra castaneiventris* Finsch and Hartlaub, Beitr. Fauna Cent., Orn., p. 95 (Upolu Island, Samoa = Viti Levu, Fiji)

Description: Male—top of head, chin, and throat glossy blue-green black; back, rump, and wing-coverts gray; wings and tail black; breast dark burnt orange, breast paler. Female—upperparts dull gray; chin and upper throat white, rest of underparts pale ochre.

Soft Parts: Bill bluish; iris brown; feet black.

Measurements: Wing ♂ 74, ♀ 70; tail ♂ 57, ♀ 54; bill 18; tarsus 17.

Range: Fiji (Asawa Ilau, Kio, Koro, Malake, Malolo, Matathawa Levu, Mathuata, Mbatiki, Monuriki, Nairai, Namenalala, Nathula, Navandra, Naviti, Ngualilo, Ovalau, Rambi, Taveuni, Thikombia, Thombia, Vanua Levu, Viti Levu, Viwa, Wakaya, Waya, Yandua, Yanutha, Yasawa)

Myiagra vanikorensis kandavensis Mayr, 1933

1933 *Myiagra vanikorensis kandavensis* Mayr, Am. Mus. Novit., 651:9 (Kandavu, Fiji)

Description: Differs from *M. v. rufiventris* as follows: Male— back and rump darker like the head; burnt orange of the breast and belly darker and richer. Female—upper and lower parts much darker.

Range: Fiji (Kandavu, Mbengga, Mbulia, Ndravuni, Ono, Vanua Kula, Vatulele, Yaukuve Lailai, Yaukuve Levu)

Myiagra vanikorensis dorsalis Mayr, 1933

1933 *Myiagra vanikorensis dorsalis* Mayr, Am. Mus. Novit., 651:9 (Matuku Island, Fiji)

Description: Differs from *M. v. kandavensis* by being uniformly darker in color.

Range: Fiji (Avea, Mango, Matuku, Moala, Munia, Naitaumba, Sovu Islets, Thithia, Totoya, Vanuambalavu, Vatavara, Welangilala, Yathata)

Myiagra vanikorensis townsendi Wetmore, 1919

1919 *Myiagra townsendi* Wetmore, Bull. Mus. Comp. Zool., **63**:205 (Kambara Island, Lau Archipelago, Fiji)

Description: Differs from other races by being darker; having the glossy black of the throat extending to the upper breast; and, most importantly, being larger (wing ♂ 76, ♀ 73; tail ♂ 65, ♀ 63).

Range: Fiji (Aiwa, Fulanga, Kambara, Komo, Lakemba, Mothe, Namu-ka-I-Lau, Oneata, Ongea Levu, Vanuavatu, Wanggava, Yangasalevu)

Remarks: This is a common bird of open areas; it may be found in gardens as well as at the edges of forests.

SAMOAN BROADBILL   PLATE 27

Myiagra albiventris (Peale, 1848)

1848   *Platyrhynchus albiventris* Peale, U. S. Expl. Expd., **8:**102 (Upolu, Samoa)

Description: Male—top of head black with a blue gloss; back and rump dark gray glossed with green; wings and tail black; chin and throat burnt orange; breast, belly, and under tail-coverts white. Female—upperparts grayer, black not so intense; chin and throat paler. Immature—similar to adults but duller.

Soft Parts: Bill bluish black; iris brown; feet black.

Measurements: Wing ♂ 72, ♀ 69; tail ♂ 62, ♀ 58; bill 17; tarsus 16.

Range: Western Samoa (Savaii, Upolu)

Remarks: This is a bird of the forests from seacoast to mountain tops. Not shy, the species usually forages and perches solitarily within 50 feet of the ground.

BLUE-CRESTED BROADBILL   PLATE 27

Myiagra azureocapilla azureocapilla Layard, 1875

1875   *Myiagra azureocapilla* Layard, Ibis, p. 434 (Taviuni, Fiji)

Description: Male—top of head and ear-coverts pale blue; forehead, lores, and stripe behind eye blackish; back, rump, and wing-coverts dark slate-blue; wings and tail black with dark blue edges; chin and throat dark chestnut; rest of underparts white. Female—crown gray; upperparts dark rufous brown; chin and throat whitish; chestnut band across upper breast. Immature—similar to female but duller.

Soft Parts: Bill orange; iris brown; feet grayish.

Measurements: Wing ♂ 83, ♀ 79; tail ♂ 72, ♀ 69; bill 17; tarsus 21.
Range: Fiji (Taveuni)

Myiagra azureocapilla castaneigularis Layard, 1876

1876   *Myiagra castaneigularis* Layard, Ibis, p. 389 (Kandi, Vanua Levu, Fiji)

Description: Differs from *M. a. azureocapilla* as follows: Male—rectrices tipped with white, the chin and throat lighter chestnut, and the breast and belly purer white. Female—back more olivaceous, rectrices tipped with white, and the chin and throat paler chestnut. Both sexes also smaller (wing ♂ 75, ♀ 75; tail ♂ 66, ♀ 66).
Range: Fiji (Vanua Levu)

Myiagra azureocapilla whitneyi Mayr, 1933

1933   *Myiagra azureocapilla whitneyi* Mayr, Am. Mus. Novit., 651:16 (Viti Levu, Fiji)

Description: Differs from *M. a. castaneigularis* by having the rectrices with reduced white tips and the chin and throat darker chestnut. Also smaller (wing ♂ 73, ♀ 73; tail ♂ 65, ♀ 60).
Range: Fiji (Viti Levu)

Remarks: This broadbill is a bird of the mountain forest and is often seen sitting on branches underneath the tops of tall trees. One bird of unidentified subspecies has been recorded from Kandavu.

KANDAVU FANTAIL   PLATE 26

Rhipidura personata Ramsay, 1876

1876   *Rhipidura personata* Ramsay, Proc. Linn. Soc. New South Wales, 1:43 (Kandavu Island, Fiji)

Description: Top of head and neck dark gray-brown; eyebrow white; back and wings dark brown; tail black, outer rectrices tipped with white; underparts white, throat with a brownish black band and belly with a light buffy wash.
Soft Parts: Bill black; iris brown; feet brown.
Measurements: Wing ♂ 85, ♀ 80; tail ♂ 91, ♀ 88; bill 12; tarsus 18.
Range: Fiji (Kandavu)

Remarks: A retiring bird of the brushy creek beds, it is often found in groups.

PLATE 25

PLATE 25

PLATE 26

PLATE 26

SANDSTRÖM

PLATE 27

PLATE 27

SANDSTRÖM

SPOTTED FANTAIL   PLATE 26

Rhipidura spilodera layardi Salvadori, 1877

1875   *Rhipidura albogularis* Layard, Proc. Zool. Soc. London, p. 29 (Ovalau
       Island, Fiji)
1877   *Rhipidura layardi* Salvadori, Ibis, p. 143 (new name for *Rhipidura albogu-
       laris,* preoccupied)

Description: Upperparts dull grayish brown; short eyebrow and ear
tuft white; tail blackish with white tips to outer rectrices; chin and upper
throat white; lower throat and breast white streaked with brown; belly
and flanks rufous-buff.
Soft Parts: Bill, upper mandible black, lower mandible horn; iris
brown; feet brownish.
Measurements: Wing ♂ 82, ♀ 79; tail ♂ 90, ♀ 85; bill 7; tarsus 19.
Range: Fiji (Ovalau, Viti Levu)

Rhipidura spilodera erythronota Sharpe, 1879

1879   *Rhipidura erythronota* Sharpe, Cat. Bds. Brit. Mus., 4:307 (in key), 337
       (Vanua Levu, Fiji)

Description: Differs from *R. s. layardi* by having the back and wings
more rufous and the head contrasting with the back.
Range: Fiji (Kio, Vanua Levu, Yangganga)

Rhipidura spilodera rufilateralis Sharpe, 1879

1876   *Rhipidura albicollis* Layard, Ibis, p. 149 (Taviuni Island) (*nomen nudum,*
       also preoccupied)
1879   *Rhipidura rufilateralis* Sharpe, Cat. Bds. Brit. Mus., 4:307 (in key), 337
       (N'gila, Taviuni)

Description: Differs from *R. s. layardi* by having the back lighter brown,
the breast with fewer streaks, and the flanks dark rufous.
Range: Fiji (Taveuni, Vanua Levu)

Remarks: A common bird of the lowlands, this species may be found
from gardens to the dense original forest.

SAMOAN FANTAIL   PLATE 26

Rhipidura nebulosa nebulosa Peale, 1848

1848   *Rhipidura nebulosa* Peale, U. S. Expl. Expd., 8:99 (Upolu, Samoa)
1876   *Rhipidura fuscescens* Cabanis and Reichenow, Journ. f. Orn., 24:319 (Se-
       gaar Bay, New Guinea = Upolu, Samoa)

Description: Entire bird sooty gray except for a white spot over the eye and the ear tufts, which are also white; rectrices with white margins; belly buffy; under tail-coverts white.

Soft Parts: Bill, upper mandible black, lower mandible horn; iris horn; feet black.

Measurements: Wing ♂ 74, ♀ 71; tail ♂ 80, ♀ 77; bill 11; tarsus 18.

Range: Western Samoa (Upolu)

Rhipidura nebulosa altera Mayr, 1931

1931 *Rhipidura nebulosa altera* Mayr, Am. Mus. Novit., 502:13 (Savaii Island, Samoa)

Description: Differs from *R. n. nebulosa* by having the white over the eye and ear tufts more pronounced, the buff of the belly more extended, and the white margins of the rectrices reduced in length but wider.

Range: Western Samoa (Savaii)

Remarks: This bird is found above 3000 feet to mountain tops, often in the middle stratum of the forest canopy where its chirps give its location away. It is commonly found in pairs.

GOLDEN WHISTLER   PLATE 28

Pachycephala pectoralis kandavensis Ramsay, 1876

1876 *Pachycephala kandavensis* Ramsay, Proc. Linn. Soc. New South Wales, 1:65 (Kandavu, Fiji)

Description: Male—top and sides of head black; narrow nuchal collar yellow; rest of upperparts dark olive; chin and throat white bordered by a black collar; breast, belly, flanks, and under tail-coverts yellow. Female—upperparts dark olive-brown; chin and throat pinkish cinnamon, rest of underparts buffy cinnamon. Immature—similar to female but strongly washed with olive.

Soft Parts: Bill black; iris brown; feet brownish.

Measurements: Wing ♂ 89, ♀ 87; tail ♂ 66, ♀ 65; bill 17; tarsus 23.

Range: Fiji (Kandavu, Mbengga, Ono, Vanua Kula)

Pachycephala pectoralis vitiensis G. R. Gray, 1859

1859 *Pachycephala vitiensis* G. R. Gray, Cat. Bds. Trop. Isl. Pac., p. 20 (Ngau, Fiji)

Description: Differs from *P. p. kandavensis* as follows: Male—tail black, black breast band wider, and yellow underparts much richer. Female—much richer ochraceous.

Range: Fiji (Ngau)

Pachycephala pectoralis lauana Mayr, 1932

1932   *Pachycephala pectoralis lauana* Mayr, Am. Mus. Novit., 531:12 (Ongea Levu, Lau Archipelago, Fiji)

Description: Differs from *P. p. vitiensis* as follows: Male—back blackish olive. Female—paler below, belly very pale buffy white.

Range: Fiji (southern Lau Archipelago: Fulanga, Ongea Levu, Wanggava)

Pachycephala pectoralis bella Mayr, 1932

1932   *Pachycephala pectoralis bella* Mayr, Am. Mus. Novit., 531:14 (Vatu Vara Island)

Description: Differs from *P. p. lauana* as follows: Male—orange-yellow supraloral spots, back more olive, chin and throat golden yellow. Female —rufous-brown, paler underparts.

Range: Fiji (Vatuvara)

Pachycephala pectoralis koroana Mayr, 1932

1932   *Pachycephala pectoralis koroana* Mayr, Am. Mus. Novit., 531:15 (Koro, Fiji)

Description: Differs from *P. p. bella* as follows: Male—lacks orange-yellow spot on either side of forehead; chin and throat richer golden yellow. Female—uniformly darker.

Range: Fiji (Koro)

Pachycephala pectoralis torquata Layard, 1875

1875   *Pachycephala torquata* Layard, Proc. Zool. Soc. London, p. 150 (Taviuni Island, Fiji)

Description: Differs from *P. p. koroana* as follows: Male—breast band narrower and underparts slightly paler. Female—similar but in a long series tends to be more rufous.

Range: Fiji (Taveuni)

Pachycephala pectoralis ambigua Mayr, 1932

1932   *Pachycephala pectoralis ambigua* Mayr, Am. Mus. Novit., 531:16 (Rambi Island, Fiji)

Description: Differs from *P. p. torquata* as follows: Male—less black in the back; chin and throat paler orange-yellow and breast band narrower. Female—upperparts more rufous, lower parts brownish.

Range: Fiji (Kio, Natewa Peninsula of Vanua Levu, Rambi)

Pachycephala pectoralis optata Hartlaub, 1866

1866   *Pachycephala (?) optata* Hartlaub, Ibis, p. 172 (Ovalau Island)

1876   *Pachycephala intermedia* Layard, Ibis, p. 154 (Tai Levu, northeastern Viti Levu)

1879 *Pachycephala neglecta* Layard, Proc. Zool. Soc. London, p. 147 (Ovalau Island)

Description: Differs from *P. p. ambigua* as follows: Male—upperparts more olive, orange-yellow of underparts more yellowish, and breast band reduced so that it is almost indistinct. Female—variable and not diagnostic.

Range: Fiji (Ovalau, northeast coast of Viti Levu)

Pachycephala pectoralis graeffii Hartlaub, 1866

1866 *Pachycephala graeffii* Hartlaub, Ibis, p. 172 (Viti Levu, Fiji)

Description: Differs from *P. p. optata* as follows: Male—has two yellow supraloral spots and lacks a complete black necklace; however, the bases of the feathers are black and in the hand an indistinct "necklace" shows through from beneath. Female—underparts much grayer and slightly mottled with black.

Range: Fiji (Viti Levu, Waya)

Pachycephala pectoralis aurantiiventris Seebohm, 1891

1891 *Pachycephala aurantiiventris* Seebohm, Ibis, pp. 94, 96 (Bua, Vanua Levu Island, Fiji)

Description: Differs from *P. p. graeffii* as follows: Male—supraloral spots larger, back darker olive, breast band almost nonexistent, and yellow-orange darker. Female—no distinct characters.

Range: Fiji (Vanua Levu [except southeastern peninsula], Yangganga)

Remarks: A bird of the rain forest, it is often seen in small flocks of eight to 20.

TONGA WHISTLER   PLATE 28

Pachycephala jacquinoti Bonaparte, 1850

1850 *Pachycephala jacquinoti* Bonaparte, Consp. Av., 1:329 (Vavao, Tonga Islands)*

1853 *Eopsaltria melanops* Pucheran, Voy. Pole Sud, Zool., 3:56 (Vavao, Tonga Islands)

---

*Some authors maintain that *Pachycephala jacquinoti* Bonaparte is a *nomen nudum* and therefore call this species *Pachycephala melanops* Pucheran. Although it is true that Bonaparte did not give a description of *jacquinoti,* he attached the name to a reference to a published figure of the bird, and this suffices to make the name available under Article 16 of the International Code of Zoological Nomenclature.

Description: Male—head, chin, and throat black; nuchal collar yellow; back and wing-coverts olive; wings and tail brownish black, rectrices tipped with yellow; breast, belly, flanks, and under tail-coverts golden yellow. Female—top of head gray-brown; back dull olive; wings dark brown with rufous edges; tail dark olive tipped with rufous; chin and throat buffy white; rest of underparts pale yellow. Immature—duller than adults but somewhat resembles female.
Soft Parts: Bill black; iris brown; feet grayish.
Measurements: Wing ♂ 103, ♀ 97; tail ♂ 71, ♀ 68; bill 19; tarsus 25.
Range: Tonga (Ava, Euakafa, Kapa, Late, Vavau)

Remarks: A bird of the low scrub of original forest, it is locally quite common.

SAMOAN WHISTLER   PLATE 28

Pachycephala flavifrons (Peale, 1848)

1848 *Eopsaltria flavifrons* Peale, U. S. Expl. Expd., **8**:96 (Upolu, Samoa)
1848 *Eopsaltria icteroides* Peale, U. S. Expl. Expd., **8**:97 (Samoa)
1848 *Eopsaltria albifrons* Peale, U. S. Expl. Expd., **8**:97 (Samoa)
1850 *Pachycephala hombroni* Bonaparte, Consp. Av., **1**:329 (Samoa)
1853 *Eopsaltria diademata* Pucheran, Voy. Pole Sud, Zool., **3**:55 (Samoa)

Description: There are three distinct color phases of this species that interbreed and can all be found in the same tree at the same time.
Phase I: Male—forehead and supraloral stripe yellow; upperparts black with a slight olive wash; wings and tail black; feathers of chin and throat dark gray with yellow tips; breast, belly, and under tail-coverts dark yellow. Female—yellow of forehead and supraloral stripe grayish yellow. Immature—similar to female but lower parts paler.
Phase II: Differs by having tips of feathers on throat white.
Phase III: Differs by having tips of the forehead and throat white.
Soft Parts: Bill black; iris brown; feet grayish.
Measurements: Wing ♂ 87, ♀ 83; tail ♂ 59, ♀ 56; bill 18; tarsus 25.
Range: Western Samoa (Savaii, Upolu)

Remarks: This bird may be found from seacoasts to mountain tops and ranges from low scrub to tree tops. It travels in groups of four to 10.

SAMOAN WHITE-EYE   PLATE 27

Zosterops samoensis Murphy and Mathews, 1929

1929   *Zosterops samoensis* Murphy and Mathews, Am. Mus. Novit., 356:11 (Savaii)

Description: Upperparts yellowish olive, rump and upper tail-coverts paler; primaries and tail brownish black; lores dirty yellow; eye-ring white; chin and upper throat light yellow; rest of underparts white washed with yellow, flanks somewhat greener.
Soft Parts: Bill brownish; iris light yellow; feet grayish.
Measurements: Wing ♂ 59, ♀ 57; tail ♂ 37, ♀ 36; bill 11; tarsus 16.
Range: Western Samoa (Savaii)

Remarks: This bird inhabits the tops of trees at elevations above 4500 feet. Its habit of traveling in flocks of 10 to 40 birds makes it very easy to find because the birds are quite vocal.

LAYARD'S WHITE-EYE   PLATE 27

Zosterops explorator Layard, 1875

1875   *Zosterops explorator* Layard, Proc. Zool. Soc. London, p. 29 (Kandavu, Fiji)

Description: Upperparts uniform olive-yellow; primaries and tail blackish brown; eye-ring white, lower half bordered with black; chin, throat, and breast yellow; belly gray-white lightly washed with yellow; under tail-coverts yellow.
Soft Parts: Bill blackish brown, base horn; iris brown; feet gray.
Measurements: Wing ♂ 61, ♀ 60; tail ♂ 35, ♀ 35; bill 12; tarsus 18.
Range: Fiji (Kandavu, Ovalau, Taveuni, Vanua Levu, Viti Levu)

Remarks: A bird of the hills and mountains, it is found above 2500 feet, often in small flocks.

158

PLATE 28

A

B

C

D

E

F

G

H

SANDSTRÖM

PLATE 28

GRAY-BACKED WHITE-EYE   PLATE 27

Zosterops lateralis flaviceps Peale, 1848

1848   *Zosterops flaviceps* Peale, U. S. Expl. Expd., **8**:95 (Vanua Levu, Fiji)

1876   *Zosterops caerulescens* var. *kandavensis* Ramsay, Proc. Linn. Soc. New South Wales, **1**:71 (Kandavu)

1925   *Zosterops lateralis mugga* Mathews, Bull. Brit. Orn. Cl., **45**:86 (new name for *Zosterops flaviceps* Finsch and Hartlaub, 1867, Beitr. Fauna Cent., Orn., p. 52 [Viti Levu], erroneously thought not to be *flaviceps* Peale, 1848)

Description: Top of head and hind neck dark olive; back gray washed with olive; eye-ring white, lower half bordered with black; rump and upper tail-coverts olive-yellow; primaries and tail brownish black; chin and throat yellow; breast grayish; belly whitish with buffy flanks.

Soft Parts: Bill light brown; iris brown; feet light brown to gray.

Measurements: Wing ♂ 60, ♀ 59; tail ♂ 44, ♀ 43; bill 11; tarsus 18.

Range: Fiji (Kandavu, Kioa, Koro, Makongai, Malake, Mbatiki, Mbeng-ga, Moala, Nairai, Namenalala, Nathula, Naviti, Ngau, Ovalau, Rambi, Taveuni, Vanua Kula, Vanua Levu, Vatulele, Viti Levu, Viwa, Vuro, Wakaya, Waya, Yandua, Yanuya, Yasawa, Yaukuve Levu)

Remarks: This is an endemic bird of the lowlands, especially the open country, where it travels in small groups.

Zosterops lateralis lateralis (Latham, 1801)

1801   *Sylvia lateralis* Latham, Ind. Orn., suppl., p. 55 (Tasmania? or mainland)

Description: Differs from *Z. l. flaviceps* by having the upperparts duller green, underparts whiter, and flanks more cinnamon.

Range: Introduced from New Zealand to the Society Islands (Bora-Bora, Moorea, Raiatea, Tahiti).

Remarks: This well-established bird is commonly found from the sea-coast to the mountains.

CARDINAL HONEY-EATER   PLATE 29

Myzomela cardinalis nigriventris Peale, 1848

1848   *Myzomela nigriventris* Peale, U. S. Expl. Expd., **8**:150 (Upolu Island, Samoa)

1889   *Myzomela rubro-cucullata* Tristram, Ibis, p. 228 (St. Aignan; error = Samoa Islands)

Description: Male—head, back, rump, upper tail-coverts, chin, throat, and upper breast red; lores, wings, tail, lower breast, and belly black. Female—entire bird dark olive-gray, paler underneath; only lower back and rump being red. Immatures—similar to females but with reduced red patches.

Soft Parts: Bill black; iris gray; feet black.

Measurements: Wing ♂ 68, ♀ 62; tail ♂ 44, ♀ 39; bill 17; tarsus 19.

Range: American Samoa (Tutuila)
          Western Samoa (Savaii, Upolu)

Remarks: A common bird of both open country and dense forest, it has been recorded from sea level to the mountain tops.

ROTUMA HONEY-EATER   PLATE 29

Myzomela chermesina G. R. Gray, 1846

1846   *Myzomela chermesina* G. R. Gray, Gen. Bds., **1**, pl. 38 (no locality = Rotuma Island)

Description: Male—back, rump, throat, breast, and flanks red; rest of bird black. Female—similar to male but red areas duller and reduced in size. Immature—similar to female but red areas reduced and black is a brownish black.

Soft Parts: Bill black; iris brown; feet black.

Measurements: Wing ♂ 77, ♀ 70; tail ♂ 54, ♀ 48; bill 16; tarsus 19.

Range: Rotuma

Remarks: A bird of the open lands and forest, it is most often found around flowering trees.

PLATE 29

PLATE 29

ORANGE-BREASTED HONEY-EATER   PLATE 29

Myzomela jugularis Peale, 1848

1848   *Myzomela jugularis* Peale, U. S. Expl. Expd., **8**:150 (Vanua Leva Island, Fiji)

1853   *Myzomela solitaria* Pucheran, Voy. Pole Sud, Zool., **3**:99 (Solomon Islands = Fiji Islands)

Description: Male—crown and hind neck red; forehead, face, and back black; lower back, rump, and upper tail-coverts red; chin and upper throat red, lower throat black; breast yellow-orange, rest of underparts yellow-white; wings black, primaries and secondaries edged with olive, wing-coverts tipped with white; tail black, rectrices tipped with white. Female—similar to male but red patches smaller and duller; black of upperparts not so intense; all of underparts yellowish white. Immature —similar to female but duller.

Soft Parts: Bill black; iris brown; feet gray-black.

Measurements: Wing ♂ 62, ♀ 58; tail ♂ 39, ♀ 35; bill ♂ 19, ♀ 17; tarsus 17.

Range: Fiji (Fulanga, Kambara, Kandavu, Katafanga, Komo, Koro, Lakemba, Leleuvia, Makongai, Mango, Matathawa Levu, Matuku, Mbatiki, Moala, Monariki, Mothe, Namenalala, Namuka-I-Lau, Nathula, Naviti, Ndravuni, Olorua, Oneata, Ongea Levu, Ovalau, Rambi, Tavunasithi, Thikombia-I-Lau, Thithia, Totoya, Vanua Kula, Vanuambalavu, Vanuavatu, Vatoa, Viti Levu, Viwa, Wakaya, Wanggava, Waya, Yangasalevu, Yanuya, Yasawa, Yaukuve Levu)

Remarks: This is a common bird of the open country and forests.

WATTLED HONEY-EATER   PLATE 29

Foulehaio carunculata carunculata (Gmelin, 1788)

1788   *Certhia carunculata* Gmelin, Syst. Nat., **1**:472 (Tongatabu)

1826   *Creadion tabuensis* Stephens, in Shaw's Gen. Zool., **14**:233 (new name for *Certhia carunculata* Gmelin, 1788)

1826   *Philemon musicus* Vieillot, Dict. Sci. Nat., **39**:480 (Tongatabu)

1876   *Ptilotis flavo-aurita* Layard, Ibis, p. 148 (Fortuna Island)

Description: Male—upperparts olive-green; ear-coverts yellowish; wings and tail dark brown edged with olive-yellow; underparts olive-gray with under tail-coverts being grayer. Female—similar to male but underparts washed with olive-yellow.

Soft Parts: Bill black; iris brown; wattles and base of lower mandible orange-yellow; feet dark gray.

Measurements: Wing ♂ 100, ♀ 90; tail ♂ 85, ♀ 72; bill 19; tarsus 29.

Range: American Samoa (Ofu, Olosega, Tau, Tutuila)

Fiji (Aiwa, Fulanga, Lakemba, Marambo, Matuku, Mothe, Nayau, Oneata, Ongea Levu, Ono-I-Lau, Tuvutha, Vanuambalavu, Vatuvara, Yathata)

Horne Islands (Alofi, Futuna)

Tonga (Eua, Euakafa, Fakahiku, Fonoifua, Fonuaika, Fonualei, Fotuhaa, Haafeva, Haano, Hunga Haapai, Kao, Kapa, Kelefesia, Late, Lua Hoko, Mango, Maninita, Moungaone, Nomuka, Nomuka Iki, Ofolanga, Oua, Pepea, Teaupa, Telekiaapai, Telekivavau, Tofonga, Tofua, Toku, Tongatapu, Tonumea, Tungua, Uiha, Uoleva, Uonuku Hahake, Vavau)

Western Samoa (Savaii, Upolu)

Foulehaio carunculata procerior (Finsch and Hartlaub, 1867)

1867   *Ptilotis procerior* Finsch and Hartlaub, Beitr. Fauna Cent., Orn., p. 62 (Ovalau Island, Fiji)

Description: Differs from *F. c. carunculata* by having the feathers of the crown and back edged with black, giving an overall darker appearance; malar streak black; feathers of throat and breast have black shaft streaks and edges, giving a scaled appearance; underparts grayer.

Range: Fiji (Kandavu, Nathula, Ovalau, Vatulele, Vawa, Viti Levu, Yasawa)

Foulehaio carunculata taviunensis (Wiglesworth, 1891)

1876   *Ptilotis similis* Layard, Ibis, p. 148 (Taviuni Island, Fiji)

1891   *Ptilotis procerior taviunensis* Wiglesworth, Abh. Ber. Mus. Dresden, **3**:34 (new name for *Ptilotis similis* Layard, 1876, preoccupied)

1891   *Ptilotis procerior buaensis* Wiglesworth, Abh. Ber. Mus. Dresden, **3**:34 (Vanua Levu Island, Fiji)

Description: Differs from *F. c. procerior* by having the malar streak gray-black; feathers of throat and breast lack black shaft streaks and edges, giving a uniform gray-green appearance.

Range: Fiji (Mathuata, Nggamea, Rambi, Taveuni, Vanua Levu, Yangganga)

Remarks: A common bird at the edges of forests and in dense jungle, it has been recorded from sea level to mountain tops.

KANDAVU HONEY-EATER   PLATE 29

Foulehaio provocator (Layard, 1875)

1875   *Ptilotis provocator* Layard, Proc. Zool. Soc. London, p. 28 (Kandavu Island, Fiji)
1876   *Ptilotis xanthophrys* Finsch, Journ. Mus. Godeffroy, **4**:5 (Fiji)

Description: Top of head olive-brown becoming darker on forehead; back olive-brown with light shaft streaks; wings and tail brown; wide circle around eye and ear-coverts golden yellow; malar stripe blackish brown; underparts dark gray, feathers with light shaft streaks.
Soft Parts: Bill black; iris brown; feet greenish.
Measurements: Wing ♂ 106, ♀ 87; tail ♂ 79, ♀ 69; bill ♂ 21, ♀ 18; tarsus 30.
Range: Fiji (Kandavu)

Remarks: This is a common bird of the scrub and forest throughout Kandavu.

GIANT FOREST HONEY-EATER   PLATE 29

Gymnomyza viridis viridis (Layard, 1875)

1875   *Tatare (?) viridis* Layard, Proc. Zool. Soc. London, p. 150 (Taveuni Island, Fiji)

Description: Entire bird olive-green, outer edges of primaries and rectrices lighter olive-green.
Soft Parts: Bill yellow; iris brown; feet yellow.
Measurements: Wing ♂ 145, ♀ 124; tail ♂ 120, ♀ 104; bill 32; tarsus 35.
Range: Fiji (Taveuni, Vanua Levu)

Gymnomyza viridis brunneirostris (Mayr, 1932)

1932   *Amoromyza viridis brunneirostris* Mayr, Am. Mus. Novit., **516**:3 (Viti Levu Island, Fiji)

Description: Differs from *G. v. viridis* by being lighter olive-green; bill and feet blackish brown, not yellow; bill smaller (30) and tail longer (♂ 127, ♀ 113).
Range: Fiji (Viti Levu)

Remarks: A bird of tall trees of the mountain forest, it is usually found above 1500 feet. It is said to creep on tree trunks.

MAO   PLATE 29

Gymnomyza samoensis (Hombron and Jacquinot, 1814)

1814   *Merops samoensis* Hombron and Jacquinot, Ann. Sci. Nat., **16**:314 (Samoa Islands = Upolu Island)

1848   *Entomiza (?) olivacea* Peale, U.S. Expl. Expd., **8**:145 (Upolu Island)

1852   *Philedon leptornis* Reichenbach, Handb. Spec. Orn., **1**:141 (Oceania = Samoa)

1853   *Leptornis sylvestris* Pucheran, Voy. Pole Sud, Zool., **3**:86 (Samoa)

Description: Top of head, chin, and upper throat dark olive-black; stripe beneath eye and ear-coverts olive; back and tail olive-brown, rump and upper tail-coverts somewhat lighter; breast and belly dark olive-brown; under tail-coverts brownish.

Soft Parts: Bill black; iris brown; feet black, soles yellow.

Measurements: Wing ♂ 148, ♀ 134; tail ♂ 137, ♀ 121; bill 43; tarsus 46.

Range: American Samoa (Tutuila)
            Western Samoa (Savaii, Upolu)

Remarks: This bird is found above 3000 feet in mountain forests. It feeds in tree tops and is very shy.

ESTRILDIDAE   GRASS FINCHES,
                                    MANNIKINS, WAXBILLS

Many members of this large family of finches have been introduced to the South Pacific, mainly to Fiji, the Society Islands, and the Marquesas. The exact date of introduction is often difficult to establish; however, it is known that Eastham and Carrie Guild introduced some 50–55 species to Tahiti in the 1920's, most of which did not establish themselves. Only those species that have established populations are treated here, but one must recognize that a small remanent population of one or the other introduced species may still exist in some isolated areas. The members of the genus *Erythrura* are native to the South Pacific.

COMMON WAXBILL   PLATE 30

Estrilda astrild ssp. (Linnaeus, 1758)

1758   *Loxia Astrild* Linnaeus, Syst. Nat., **1**:73 (Canaries, America, Africa = Cape Town)

Description: Upperparts gray-brown barred with dark brown; tail dark brown; lores and stripe behind eye red; underparts pale gray-brown barred with dark brown and washed with red on the throat and breast, becoming a central stripe on the belly; under tail-coverts black.
Soft Parts: Bill red; iris brown; feet black.
Measurements: Wing ♂ 47, ♀ 49; tail ♂ 45, ♀ 46; bill 8.5; tarsus 12.
Range: Introduced from Africa to the Society Islands (Moorea, Tahiti).

Remarks: A common bird of the open areas, it is usually found in small groups of four to 10.

WEAVERBIRD   **PLATE 30**

Aegintha temporalis temporalis (Latham, 1801)

1801   *Fringilla temporalis* Latham, Ind. Orn., suppl., p. 48 (New Holland = Sydney, New South Wales)

Description: Forehead, crown, and cheeks gray; lores and eye-stripe red; patches on sides of neck dull golden green; back and wings dark olive; rump and upper tail-coverts bright red; tail dark brownish black; chin whitish; throat and breast gray; belly buff; under tail-coverts gray.
Soft Parts: Bill, upper mandible red, lower mandible red; iris brown; feet flesh color.
Measurements: Wing ♂ 53, ♀ 54; tail ♂ 46, ♀ 47; bill 10; tarsus 13.
Range: Introduced from Australia to the Society Islands (Moorea, Tahiti).

Remarks: Commonly seen around towns and in the open countryside, this bird often travels in flocks of 10 to 20.

STRAWBERRY FINCH   **PLATE 30**

Amandava amandava ssp. (Linnaeus, 1758)

1758   *Fringilla amandava* Linnaeus, Syst. Nat., **1**:180 (Calcutta)
Description: Male—top of head mottled olive and dark red; back olive-brown; upper tail-coverts dark red; tail black; wing-coverts dark brown with white spots; underparts bright red with fine white spots on sides of

breast and flanks. Female—upperparts olive-brown; chin and throat whitish; rest of underparts buffy.

Soft Parts: Bill bright red; iris orange-red; feet pale brown.

Measurements: Wing ♂ 53, ♀ 52; tail ♂ 36, ♀ 36; bill 9; tarsus 12.

Range: Introduced from Southern Asia to Fiji (Taveuni, Vanua Levu, Viti Levu).

Remarks: A common bird of the open lowlands, especially rice fields and other grassy areas, it often travels in large flocks.

RED-HEADED PARROT-FINCH   PLATE 30

Erythrura cyaneovirens cyaneovirens (Peale, 1848)

1848   *Geospiza cyaneovirens* Peale, U. S. Expl. Expd., **8**:117 (Upolu, Samoa)

1850   *Erythrura pucherani* Bonaparte, Consp. Av., **1**:457 (Oceania = Upolu, Samoa)

1870   *Lobiospiza notabilis* Hartlaub and Finsch, Proc. Zool. Soc. London, p. 817 (Upolu, Samoa)

Description: Forehead, crown, sides of face, and nape red; back and wings blue-green; upper tail-coverts and tail reddish maroon; chin, throat, and upper breast bluish; rest of underparts green. Young are much duller, with bill mostly yellow.

Soft Parts: Bill blackish; iris brown; feet brown.

Measurements: Wing ♂ 64, ♀ 62; tail ♂ 37, ♀ 35; bill 12; tarsus 16.

Range: Western Samoa (Upolu)

Erythrura cyaneovirens pealii Hartlaub, 1852

1848   *Geospiza prasina* Peale, U. S. Expl. Expd., **8**:116 (Vanua Levu, Fiji)

1852   *Erythrura Pealii* Hartlaub, Arch. f. Natürg., p. 104 (new name for *Geospiza prasina* Peale, 1848, preoccupied)

Description: Differs from *E. c. cyaneovirens* by having the red on the head and tail brighter, the back greener, the chin blackish, and the green of the underparts greener.

Range: Fiji (Kandavu, Malolo, Naviti, Taveuni, Tavua, Vanua Levu, Viti Levu, Waya, Yanuya, Yasawa)

Erythrura cyaneovirens gaughrani duPont, 1972

1972   *Erythrura cyaneovirens gaughrani*, Wil. Bull., **84**:376 (Mt. 'O'a, Savaii, Western Samoa, 5000')

Description: Differs from *E. c. cyaneovirens* by having the red on the head and tail darker; blue on the nape paler and less extensive; back, wings, and underparts greener, lacking the heavy bluish wash.
Range: Western Samoa (Savaii)

Remarks: This is a bird of the low bush and floor of forests. It may be found in gardens along the seacoast to the mountain tops.

PINK-BILLED PARROT-FINCH   PLATE 30

Erythrura kleinschmidti (Finsch, 1878)

1878   *Amblynura kleinschmidti* Finsch, Proc. Zool. Soc. London, p. 440 (Viti Levu)

Description: Face black; central and hind part of crown bluish; back and wings green; rump and upper tail-coverts bright red; tail dark brown; underparts green; sides of face, especially ear-coverts, brighter.
Soft Parts: Bill pinkish yellow; iris red; feet light purple.
Measurements: Wing ♂ 66, ♀ 69; tail ♂ 35, ♀ 34; bill 17; tarsus 20.
Range: Fiji (Viti Levu)

Remarks: A bird of the open areas around rice fields, it may be found in flocks of 10 to 25. It is often overlooked and sometimes considered to be other species. In the Samoas this bird has turned up as a cage pet imported from Fiji.

CHESTNUT-BREASTED FINCH   PLATE 30

Lonchura castaneothorax castaneothorax (Gould, 1837)

1837   *Amadina castaneothorax* Gould, Syn. Bds. Austr., pt. 2, pl. 21 (Australia = New South Wales)

Description: Forehead, crown, and hind neck light gray-brown, feathers with dark brown centers; back and wing-coverts dark reddish brown; rump and upper tail-coverts bright orange-brown; primaries and rectrices dark brown; face, chin, and upper throat dark brownish black; feathers of face have orange shafts; central throat buffy brown followed by a dark brownish black band separating it from the breast; breast and

belly white; under tail-coverts black. Immature—uniformly light brown with darker brown wings and tail; breast and belly creamy.
Soft Parts: Bill bluish; iris brown; feet bluish.
Measurements: Wing ♂ 56, ♀ 54; tail ♂ 33, ♀ 31; bill 11; tarsus 14.
Range: Introduced from Australia to the Society Islands (Bora-Bora, Moorea, Raiatea, Tahiti).

Remarks: A common bird of the open farm areas, it is often seen in large flocks of 20 to 50.

JAVA SPARROW   PLATE 30

Padda oryzivora (Linnaeus, 1758)

1758   *Loxia oryzivora* Linnaeus, Syst. Nat., **1**:173 (Asia and Ethiopia = Java)

Description: Top of head black; back and wings light blue-gray; rump and tail black; sides of face white; chin black; throat and breast light blue-gray; belly purplish gray; under tail-coverts white lightly washed with purple. Immature—dull gray above; cheeks and underparts pale brownish gray; bill black.
Soft Parts: Bill pink; iris brown; feet pinkish.
Measurements: Wing ♂ 64, ♀ 64; tail ♂ 41, ♀ 40; bill 16; tarsus 16.
Range: Introduced from Indonesia to Fiji (Taveuni, Vanua Levu, Viti Levu).

Remarks: Introduced in the 1930's, this is a common bird of open lowlands, especially the rice fields, as well as local gardens.

STURNIDAE   STARLINGS

SAMOAN STARLING   PLATE 31

Aplonis atrifusca (Peale, 1848)

1848   *Lamprotornis atrifusca* Peale, U. S. Expl. Expd., **8**:109 (Samoan Islands = Upolu)
1853   *Sturnoides gigas* Pucheran, Voy. Pole Sud, Zool., **3**:84 (Samoa)

Description: Entire bird very dark brown; head, chin, throat, and breast somewhat darker, somewhat iridescent.

Soft Parts: Bill black; iris dark brown; feet black.

Measurements: Wing ♂ 156, ♀ 146; tail ♂ 107, ♀ 100; bill 35; tarsus 35.

Range: American Samoa (Ofu, Olosega, Tau, Tutuila)
　　　　　Western Samoa (Savaii, Upolu)

Remarks: A common bird found from seacoast to mountain tops, it is often seen in small groups.

POLYNESIAN STARLING   PLATE 31

Aplonis tabuensis brevirostris (Peale, 1848)

1848 *Lamprotornis brevirostris* Peale, U. S. Expl. Expd., **7**:111 (Samoan Islands = Upolu)

Description: Upperparts dark brown, top of head glossed with purple; outer margins of secondaries white; underparts gray-brown with whitish shaft streaks.

Soft Parts: Bill yellowish brown; iris yellow; feet horn-brown.

Measurements: Wing ♂ 106, ♀ 101; tail ♂ 56, ♀ 53; bill 19; tarsus 26.

Range: Western Samoa (Savaii, Upolu)

Aplonis tabuensis tutuilae Mayr, 1942

1942 *Aplonis tabuensis tutuilae* Mayr, Am. Mus. Novit., 1166:2 (Tutuila)

Description: Differs from *A. t. brevirostris* by being darker, especially the underparts; also larger (wing ♂ 112, ♀ 101; tail ♂ 61, ♀ 54).

Range: American Samoa (Tutuila)

Aplonis tabuensis manuae Mayr, 1942

1942 *Aplonis tabuensis manuae* Mayr, Am. Mus. Novit., 1166:1 (Tau)

Description: Differs from *A. t. tutuilae* by having the upperparts darker, with only the slightest trace of white in the secondaries; the underparts dark gray-brown without any pale shaft streaks; also smaller (wing ♂ 108, ♀ 104; tail ♂ 59, ♀ 56).

Range: American Samoa (Ofu, Olosega, Tau)

Aplonis tabuensis brunnescens Sharpe, 1890

1890 *Aplonis brunnescens* Sharpe, Cat. Bds. Brit. Mus., **13**:126 (in key), 132 (Savage Island = Niue Island)

Description: Differs from *A. t. brevirostris* by having the upperparts browner; underparts ashy brown, shaft streaks narrower; under tail-coverts paler.
Range: Niue

Aplonis tabuensis tabuensis (Gmelin, 1788)

1788 *Lanius tabuensis* Gmelin, Syst. Nat., **1**:306 (Friendly Islands = Tonga Islands)

1836 *Aplonis marginata* Gould, Proc. Zool. Soc. London, p. 73 (Tonga Islands)

1844 *Lanius gambieranus* Lesson, Echo du Monde Sav., p. 232 (Gambier Islands)

1848 *Lamprotornis* (?) *fusca* Peale, U. S. Expl. Expd., **7**:110 (Tonga and Fiji Islands = Tongatabu)

1852 *Aplonis marginalis* Hartlaub, Arch. f. Natürg., p. 132 (new name for *fusca* Peale, 1848, preoccupied)

1859 *Aplonis cassini* G. R. Gray, Proc. Zool. Soc. London, p. 163 (new name for *fusca* Peale, 1848)

Description: Differs from *A. t. brevirostris* by having upperparts lighter brown; underparts much paler, almost buffy; brown with shaft streaks not so contrasting; also larger (wing ♂ 112, ♀ 108; tail ♂ 65, ♀ 63; bill 25).
Range: Fiji (Lau Archipelago: Ono-I-Lau, Vatoa)
Tonga (Ata, Ava, Eua, Euakafa, Foa, Fonoifua, Fotuhaa, Haa-feva, Haano, Hunga Haapai, Hunga Tonga, Kao, Kelefesia, Late, Lifuka, Mango, Moungaone, Nomuka, Nomuka Iki, Ofolanga, Oua, Teaupa, Telekiaapai, Telekitonga, Tofua, Tongatapu, Tonumea, Tungua, Uiha, Uoleva, Vavau)

Aplonis tabuensis tenebrosus Mayr, 1942

1942 *Aplonis tabuensis tenebrosus* Mayr, Am. Mus. Novit., 1166:3 (Boscawen)

Description: Differs from *A. t. tabuensis* by being almost uniformly dark sooty brown; upperparts with a greenish gloss; lower parts have very fine, buffy shaft streaks.
Measurements: Wing ♂ 112, ♀ 107; tail ♂ 64, ♀ 60.
Range: Tonga (Niuatoputapu, Tafahi)

Aplonis tabuensis nesiotes Mayr, 1942

1942   *Aplonis tabuensis nesiotes* Mayr, Am. Mus. Novit., 1166:3 (Niuafou)

Description: Differs from *A. t. tenebrosa* by being slightly lighter, the green gloss of the upperparts not so heavy, the pale shaft streaks not so conspicuous, and the belly paler.
Measurements: Wing ♂ 116, ♀ 113; tail ♂ 69, ♀ 67.
Range: Tonga (Niuafoo)

Aplonis tabuensis fortunae Layard, 1876

1876   *Aplonis fortunae* Layard, Ibis, p. 147 (Fortuna = Futuna)

Description: Differs from *A. t. tabuensis* by having the back browner; the underparts paler, especially the belly; and the shaft streaks whiter. Also smaller.
Measurements: Wing ♂ 108, ♀ 103; tail ♂ 66, ♀ 63.
Range: Horne Islands (Alofi, Futuna, Uvea)

Aplonis tabuensis rotumae Mayr, 1942

1942   *Aplonis tabuensis rotumae* Mayr, Am. Mus. Novit., 1166:4 (Rotuma)

Description: Differs from *A. t. fortunae* by having the upperparts gray-brown, the underparts grayer with wider shaft streaks, and the whitish of the belly more extensive.
Measurements: Wing ♂ 109, ♀ 103; tail ♂ 64, ♀ 60.
Range: Rotuma

Aplonis tabuensis vitiensis Layard, 1876

1876   *Aplonis vitiensis* Layard, Proc. Zool. Soc. London, p. 502 (Viti Levu, Fiji)

Description: Differs from *A. t. tabuensis* by being uniformly lighter in color, having broader shaft streaks, and being smaller.
Measurements: Wing ♂ 98–115, ♀ 98–110; tail ♂ 56–69, ♀ 55–65.
Range: Fiji. The color of the iris varies in this form. Those populations having a yellow iris: Fulanga, Kambara, Katafanga, Komo, Marambo, Mothe, Namuka-I-Lau, Nanuku Levu, Nggele Levu, Nukumbasanga, Olorua, Oneata, Ongea Levu, Sovu Islets, Tavunasithi, Tuvutha, Vanuamasi, Vanuavatu, Vatuvara, Wanggava, Yangasalevu. Those populations having a brown iris: Avea, Kandavu, Kimbombo Islands, Kio, Makongai, Matuku, Moala, Namenalala, Naviti, Nayau, Ndravuni, Ono, Ovalau, Rambi, Taveuni, Thikombia-I-Lau, Thithia, Totoya, Vanua Kula, Vatulele, Viti Levu, Wakaya, Yandua, Yasawa, Yaukuve Levu. Those populations having both colors: Aiwa, Lakemba, Mango, Munia, Naitaumba, Vanuambalavu, Vatanua, Welangilala, Yathata. Those populations having the color of the iris unknown: Ngau, Thikombia.

Remarks: A common bird of the open lands and forest, it may be found from the seacoast to the mountain tops.

MYSTERIOUS STARLING   PLATE 31

Aplonis mavornata Buller, 1887

1887   *Aplonis mavornata* Buller, 1887 (1888), Bds. New Zealand, ed. 2, p. 25 (no locality = ?Raiatea)

1890   *Aplonis inornata* Sharpe, Cat. Bds. Brit. Mus., **13**:135 (emendation of *Aplonis mavornata* Buller)

Description: Entire bird brown with a slight gloss on the head; wing primaries and tail slightly darker. As this unique specimen was on exhibit in the British Museum for many years, it may be faded.
Soft Parts: Unknown.
Measurements: Wing 106; tail 56; bill 19; tarsus 28.
Range: ?Society Islands (Raiatea). Extinct.

Remarks: This bird is known only from a unique specimen in the British Museum and is believed to have been collected somewhere in the Central or South Pacific. It has been intimated that it may have come from Raiatea in the Society Islands group.

RAROTONGA STARLING   PLATE 31

Aplonis cinerascens Hartlaub and Finsch, 1871

1871   *Aplonis cinerascens* Hartlaub and Finsch, Proc. Zool. Soc. London, p. 29 (Rarotonga)

Description: Top of head brown with a coppery gloss; mantle, rump, and upper tail-coverts gray-brown with gray margins to the feathers of the rump and upper tail-coverts; wings and tail dark brown; underparts gray-brown, becoming paler on the belly.
Soft Parts: Bill bluish slate; iris dark slate; feet bluish slate.
Measurements: Wing 123; tail 74; bill 26; tarsus 30.
Range: Cook Islands (Rarotonga)

Remarks: The habits of this bird are unknown.

PLATE 30

PLATE 30

SANDSTRÖM

PLATE 31

PLATE 31

EUROPEAN STARLING   PLATE 31

Sturnus vulgaris ssp. Linnaeus, 1758

1758   *Sturnus vulgaris* Linnaeus, Syst. Nat., **1**:67 (Sweden)

Description: Entire bird blackish; head, chin, and throat glossed with purple, rest of bird glossed with green. In freshly moulted specimens the feathers of the upperparts are tipped with buff, feathers of underparts tipped with white. Immature—uniform brownish gray.

Soft Parts: Bill yellow in breeding season, blackish brown otherwise; iris dark brown; feet dark flesh color.

Measurements: Wing ♂ 122, ♀ 120; tail ♂ 69, ♀ 66; bill 28; tarsus 27.

Range: Introduced to Fiji (southern Lau Archipelago: Ono, Vatoa, and a few outlying islands).

Remarks: This is a bird of the civilized areas and the surrounding open countryside.

COMMON MYNA   PLATE 31

Acridotheres tristis tristis (Linnaeus, 1766)

1766   *Paradisea tristis* Linnaeus, Syst. Nat., **1**:167 (Philippines; error = Pondichery)

Description: Top of head, face, and short crest black; back, rump, and wing-coverts dark brown; primaries brownish black with a white patch; rectrices black with white tips, the outer ones with the wider margins; chin and throat black; breast and belly violet-brown with a white patch in the center of the belly; under tail-coverts white.

Soft Parts: Bill yellow; iris yellow; naked patch around eye yellowish orange; feet yellowish orange.

Measurements: Wing ♂ 143, ♀ 140; tail ♂ 85, ♀ 83; bill 23; tarsus 38.

Range: Introduced from India to Fiji (Taveuni, Viti Levu).
          Society Islands (Moorea, Raiatea, Tahiti).

Remarks: This is a common bird of the open countryside and in and about towns. It is expected to spread to other islands.

JUNGLE MYNA   PLATE 31

Acridotheres fuscus fuscus (Wagler, 1827)

1827   *Pastor fuscus* Wagler, Syst. Av., *Pastor,* 6 (India = eastern Bengal)

Description: Top of head glossy black with a crest and a nasal tuft; back, rump, and wing-coverts gray-brown; wings dark brown with a white stripe; tail blackish with wide white tips to rectrices; chin, throat, and flanks dark gray; breast and belly dirty pinkish white; under tail-coverts white.

Soft Parts: Bill orange-yellow, basal third of lower mandible bluish black; iris yellow; feet orange-yellow.

Measurements: Wing ♂ 119, ♀ 120; tail ♂ 80, ♀ 79; bill 23; tarsus 36.

Range: Introduced from India to Fiji (Nukulau, Viti Levu). Expected to spread to other islands.

Remarks: A common bird of the countryside, it often travels in small groups of four to six.

ARTAMIDAE   WOOD-SWALLOWS

WHITE-BREASTED WOOD-SWALLOW   PLATE 31

Artamus leucorhynchus mentalis Jardine, 1845

1845   *Artamus mentalis* Jardine, Ann. Mag. Nat. Hist., **16**:174 (no locality = Fiji)

Description: Top of head, mantle, back, and wings black; rump white; tail black, rectrices tipped with white; chin and upper throat black; rest of underparts white.

Soft Parts: Bill bluish, tip black; iris brown; feet blackish gray.

Measurements: Wing ♂ 127, ♀ 122; tail 75; bill 23; tarsus 16.

Range: Fiji (Kio, Makongai, Malolo, Matathawa Levu, Nairai, Naviti, Navua, Nggamea, Ovalau, Rambi, Taveuni, Vanua Levu, Vawa, Viti Levu, Waya, Yandua, Yasawa)

Remarks: A common bird of the lowlands, it is often seen on wires and dead branches.

BLACK-BACKED MAGPIE   PLATE 31

Gymnorhina tibicen ssp. (Latham, 1801)

1801   C.[oracias] tibicen Latham, Ind. Orn., suppl., p. 27 (New South Wales)

Description: Male—top of head, middle of back, primaries, secondaries, terminal third of tail, chin, throat, breast, and belly black; hind neck, upper back, rump, basal two thirds of tail, wing-coverts, and under tail-coverts white. Female—similar to male but upper back and rump grayer.
Soft Parts: Bill slate; iris brown; feet black.
Measurements: Wing 256; tail 138; bill 49; tarsus 62.
Range: Introduced from Australia to Fiji (Taveuni).

Remarks: This bird is common around lowland towns.

BIBLIOGRAPHY

Alexander, W. B.
  1928 Birds of the Ocean, pp. 1-300.

Amadon, D.
  1942 Birds collected during the Whitney South Sea Expedition,
        XLIX. Notes on some non-passerine genera. Am. Mus.
        Novit., 1175:1-11.
  1942 Birds collected during the Whitney South Sea Expedition,
        L. Notes on some non-passerine genera, 2. Am. Mus.
        Novit., 1176:1-21.
  1943 Birds collected during the Whitney South Sea Expedition,
        LII. Notes on some non-passerine genera, 3. Am. Mus.
        Novit., 1237:1-22.

Amadon, D., and J. E. duPont
  1970 Notes on Philippine Birds. Nemouria, 1:1-14.

Amerson, A. Binion, Jr.
  1969 Ornithology of the Marshall and Gilbert Islands. Atoll Re-
        search Bulletin, 127:1-348.

Anker, J.
  1938 Bird Books and Bird Art. An outline of the literary his-
        tory and iconography of descriptive ornithology—based
        principally on the collection of books containing plates
        with figures of birds and their eggs now in the University
        Library at Copenhagen and including a catalogue of these
        works.

Armstrong, J. S.
  1932 Hand-list to the Birds of Samoa.

Ashmole, M. J.
  1963 Guide to the Birds of Samoa.

Bahr, P. H.
  1911 On a journey to the Fiji Islands, etc. Ibis, pp. 282-314.

Bailey, A. M., and J. H. Sorensen
  1962 Subantarctic Campbell Island, Proceedings Number 10.

Baker, R. H.
  1951 The avifauna of Micronesia: its origin, evolution, and dis-
        tribution. Univ. of Kan. Mus. Nat. His., 3:1-359.

Ball, S. C.
  1933 Jungle fowls from Pacific Islands. Bull. Bernice P. Bishop
        Museum, 108:1-121.

Beecher, W. J.
  1953   A phylogeny of the Oscines. Auk, **70**:270-333.
Belcher, W. J.
  1929   Fragmentary notes on bird life in the Fijis. Condor, **31**:1.
Belcher, W. J., and R. B. Sibson
  1972   Birds of Fiji in Colour.
Bennett, G.
  1864   Notes on the *Didunculus strigirostris* or tooth-billed
         pigeon. Proc. Zool. Soc. London, pp. 139-143.
Berlioz, J.
  1929   Les caractères de la faune avienne de Polynésie. L'Oiseau
         Rev. Fr. d'Orn., **10**:581-590.
Blackburn, A.
  1971   Some notes on Fijian birds. Notornis, **18**:147-174.
Bogert, C.
  1937   Birds collected during the Whitney South Sea Expedition,
         XXXIV. The distribution and the migration of the long-
         tailed cuckoo (*Urodynamis taitensis* Sparrman). Am. Mus.
         Novit., **933**:1-12.
Bourne, W. R. P.
  1959   A new little shearwater from the Tubuai Islands: *Puffinus
         assimilis myrtae* subsp. Emu, **59**:212-214.
Brandt, J. H.
  1962   Nests and eggs of birds of the Turk Islands. Condor,
         64:416-437.
Brown, B., and P. Child
  1975   Notes on a field trip to Fiji. Notornis, **22**:10-22.
Brown, L., and D. Amadon
  1968   Eagles, Hawks and Falcons of the World.
Bruner, P. L.
  1972   Birds of French-Polynesia, pp. i-vi, 1-135.
Burton, P. J. K.
  1974   Jaw and tongue features in Psittaciformes and other
         orders, with special reference to the anatomy of the
         tooth-billed pigeon (*Didunculus strigirostris*). Proc. Zool.
         Soc. London, **174**:255-276.

Cassin, J.
1858   United States Exploring Expedition *8,* Mammology and Ornithology [ed. 2].

Clapp, R. B., and F. C. Sibley
1966   Notes on the birds of Tutuila, American Samoa. Notornis, 13:157-164.

Clunie, F.
1972   Fijian birds of prey. Fiji Mus. Ed. Ser., 3:1-14.

Cottrell, G. W.
1968   A   problem   species: *Lamprolia   victoriae.*   Emu, 66:253-266.

Davidson, M. E. M.
1931   On the breeding of *Puffinus chlororhynchus* in the Tonga Group. Condor, 32:217-218.

Deignan, H. G.
1961   Type specimens of birds in the United States National Museum. Bull. U. S. Nat. Mus., **221**.

Dunmire, W. W.
1960   Some 1960 bird observations in Samoa and Fiji. Elepaio, 20:76-78.

duPont, J. E.
1972   Notes from Western Samoa, including the description of a new parrot-finch (*Erythrura*). Wilson Bull., 84:375-376.

Finsch, O.
1873   On *Lamprolia victoriae,* a most remarkable new passerine bird from the Feejee Islands. Proc. Zool. Soc. London, pp. 733-735.
1876   Zur Ornithologie der Südsee-Inseln. Ueber neue und weniger gekannte Vögel von den Viti, Samoa und Carolinen-Inseln. Jour. Mus. Godeffroy, 12:1-42.

Finsch, O., and G. Hartlaub
1867   Beitrage zur Fauna Centralpolynesiens, Ornithologie der Viti, Samoa und Tonga-Inseln, pp. 1-290.
1870   Ornithologie   der   Tonga-Inseln.   Journ.   f.   Orn., 18:119-140.

Fisher, A. K., and A. Wetmore
1931   Report on the birds recorded by the Pinchot Expedition

of 1929 to the Caribbean and Pacific. Proc. U. S. Nat. Mus., 79:1–66.

Fry, F. X.
   1966   Birds observed on various Polynesian islands aboard the research ship *Te Vega.* Elepaio, 27:3–5, 16–19.

Galbraith, I. C. J.
   1967   The black-tailed and robust whistlers *Pachycephala melanura* as a species distinct from the golden whistler *P. pectoralis.* Emu, 66:289–294.

Gifford, E. W.
   1925   The gray-hooded quail dove (*Gallicolumba rubescens*) of the Marquesas Islands, in captivity. Auk, 42:388–396.

Godman, F. duCane
   1907-10   A Monograph of the Petrels (Order Tubinares).

Goodwin, D.
   1967   Pigeons and Doves of the World, pp. 1–446.

Gorman, M. L.
   1975   Habitats of the land-birds of Viti Levu, Fiji Islands. Ibis, 117:152–161.

Gräffe, E.
   1870   Die Vogelwelt der Tonga Inslen. Journ. f. Orn., 18:401–420.

Gray, G. R.
   1859   Catalogue of the birds of the tropical islands of the Pacific Ocean, in the collection of the British Museum.

Greenway, J. C.
   1958   Extinct and Vanishing Birds of the World, pp. 1–518.
   1973   Type specimens of birds in the American Museum of Natural History, part 1. Bull. Am. Mus. Nat. His., 150:207–346.

Holyoak, D. T.
   1973   Notes on the birds of Rangiroa, Tuamotu Archipelago, and the surrounding ocean. Bull. Brit. Orn. Cl., 93:26–32.
   1974   Les oiseaux des Iles Societe. L'Oiseau Rev. Fr. d'Orn., 44:1–27, 153–181.
   1974   Undescribed land birds from the Cook Islands, Pacific Ocean. Bull. Brit. Orn. Cl., 94:145–150.

Jenkins, J. A. F.
1973 Seabird observations around the Kingdom of Tonga. Notornis, 20:113-119.

Keast, A.
1958 Intraspecific variation in the Australian finches. Emu, 58:219-246.

Keith, A. R.
1957 Bird observations in Fiji and Samoa, as furnished to E. H. Bryan, Jr. Elepaio, 18:25-27.

King, J. E.
1958 Some observations on the birds of Tahiti and the Marquesas Islands. Elepaio, 19:14-17.

King, W. B.
1967 Seabirds of the Tropical Pacific Ocean, pp. 1-126.

Lacan, F., and J. L. Mougin
1974 Les oiseaux des iles Gambier et de quelques atolls orientaux de l'archipel des Tuamotu (Ocean Pacifique). L'Oiseau Rev. Fr. d'Orn., 44:191-280.

Layard, E. L.
1875 Ornithological notes from Fiji, with descriptions of supposed new species of birds. Proc. Zool. Soc. London, pp. 27-30.
1875 Descriptions of some supposed new species of birds from the Fiji Islands. Proc. Zool. Soc. London, pp. 149-151.
1875 Notes on Fijian birds. Proc. Zool. Soc. London, pp. 423-442.
1876 Notes on some little-known birds of the Fiji Islands. Ibis, pp. 137-157.
1876 Description of a new species of flycatcher (*Myiagra*) from the Fijis and some remarks on the distribution of the birds found in those islands. Ibis, pp. 387-394.
1876 Notes on the birds of the Navigator's and Friendly Islands, with some additional ornithology of Fiji. Proc. Zool. Soc. London, pp. 490-506.

Lysaght, A. M.
1953 A rail from Tonga, *Rallus philippensis ecaudata* Miller, 1783. Bull. Brit. Orn. Cl., 73:74-75.
1959 Some eighteenth century bird paintings in the library of Sir Joseph Banks (1743-1820). Bull. Brit. Mus. (Nat. Hist.), Historical Series, 1:251-371.

1956   A note on the Polynesian black or sooty rail, vol. 76. Bull.
       Brit. Orn. Cl., 76:97–98.

Marshall, J. T., Jr.
1949   The endemic avifauna of Saipan, Tinian, Guam and Palau.
       Condor, 51:200–221.

Mathews, G. M.
1927   Systema Avium Australasianarum, part I, pp. 1–426.
1930   Systema Avium Australasianarum, part II, pp. 427–1048.

Mayr, E.
1931   Birds collected during the Whitney South Sea Expedition,
       XII. Notes on *Halcyon chloris* and some of its subspecies.
       Am. Mus. Novit., 469:1–10.
1931   The parrot finches (genus *Erythrura*). Am. Mus. Novit.,
       489:1–10.
1931   Birds collected during the Whitney South Sea Expedition,
       XVI. Notes on fantails of the genus *Rhipidura*. Am. Mus.
       Novit., 502:1–21.
1932   Birds collected during the Whitney South Sea Expedition,
       XVIII. Notes on *Meliphagidae* from Polynesia and the
       Solomon Islands. Am. Mus. Novit., 516:1–30.
1932   Birds collected during the Whitney South Sea Expedition,
       XXI. Notes on thickheads (*Pachycephala*) from Polynesia.
       Am. Mus. Novit., 531:1–23.
1933   Birds collected during the Whitney South Sea Expedition,
       XXIV. Notes on Polynesian flycatchers and a revision of
       the genus *Clytorhynchus* Elliot. Am. Mus. Novit.,
       628:1–21.
1933   Birds collected during the Whitney South Sea Expedition,
       XXV. Notes on the genera *Myiagra* and *Mayrornis*. Am.
       Mus. Novit., 651:1–20.
1934   Birds collected during the Whitney South Sea Expedition,
       XXIX. Notes on the genus *Petroica*. Am. Mus. Novit.,
       714:1–19.
1935   Birds collected during the Whitney South Sea Expedition,
       XXX. Descriptions of twenty-five new species and sub-
       species. Am. Mus. Novit., 820:1–6.
1936   Birds collected during the Whitney South Sea Expedition,
       XXXI. Descriptions of twenty-five species and subspecies.
       Am. Mus. Novit., 828:1–19.

1941   Birds collected during the Whitney South Sea Expedition, XLVII. Notes on the genera *Halcyon, Turdus,* and *Eurostopodus.* Am. Mus. Novit., 1152:1-7.

1942   Birds collected during the Whitney South Sea Expedition, XLVIII. Notes on the Polynesian species of *Aplonis.* Am. Mus. Novit., 1166:1-6.

1945   Birds of the Southwest Pacific.

Mayr, E., and D. Amadon

1941   Birds collected during the Whitney South Sea Expedition, XLVI. Geographical variation in *Demigretta sacra* (Gmelin). Am. Mus. Novit., 1144:1-11.

Mayr, E., and D. Ripley

1941   Birds collected during the Whitney South Sea Expedition, XLIV. Notes on the genus *Lalage* Boie. Am. Mus. Novit., 1116:1-18.

Mercer, R.

1966   A Field Guide to Fiji Birds.

Morgan, B., and J. Morgan

1965   Some notes on the birds of the Fiji Islands. Notornis, 12:158-168.

Morrison, J. P. E.

1954   Animal ecology of Raroia Atoll, Tuamotus. Atoll Research Bulletin, 34:19-26.

Murphy, R. C.

1924   Birds collected during the Whitney South Sea Expedition, I. Am. Mus. Novit., 115:1-11.

1924   Birds collected during the Whitney South Sea Expedition, II. Am. Mus. Novit., 124:1-13.

1924   Birds collected during the Whitney South Sea Expedition, III. Am. Mus. Novit., 149:1-2.

1928   Birds collected during the Whitney South Sea Expedition, IV. Am. Mus. Novit., 322:1-5.

1929   Birds collected during the Whitney South Sea Expedition, X. Am. Mus. Novit., 370:1-17.

1936   Oceanic Birds of South America.

1951   The Populations of the wedge-tailed shearwater (*Puffinus pacificus*). Am. Mus. Novit., 1512:1-21.

Murphy, R. C., and G. M. Mathews
  1928 Birds collected during the Whitney South Sea Expedition, V. Am. Mus. Novit., 337:1-18.
  1929 Birds collected during the Whitney South Sea Expedition, VI. Am. Mus. Novit., 350:1-21.
  1929 Birds collected during the Whitney South Sea Expedition, VII. Am. Mus. Novit., 356:1-14.

Murphy, R. C., and J. M. Pennoyer
  1952 Larger petrels of the genus *Pterodroma*. Am. Mus. Novit., 1580:1-43.

Murphy, R. C., and J. P. Snyder
  1952 The *"Pealea"* phenomenon and other notes on storm-petrels. Am. Mus. Novit., 1596:1-16.

Newman, T. H.
  1910 Nesting of the white-throated pigeon. Avicult. Mag., pp. 158-164, 193-195.
  1912 The white-throated pigeon. Avicult. Mag., pp. 110-115.

Oates, E. W., and S. G. Reid
  1905 Catalogue of the collection of birds' eggs in the British Museum (Natural History).

Olson, S. L.
  1973 A classification of the Rallidae. Wilson Bull., 85:381-416.
  1974 The South Pacific gallinules or the genus *Pareudiastes*. Wilson Bull., 87:1-5.

Ornithological Society of New Zealand
  1970 Annotated Checklist of the birds of New Zealand. pp. 1-96.

Peale, T. R.
  1848 United States Exploring Expedition *8*, Mammology and Ornithology [ed. 1].

Porter, S.
  1935 Notes on birds of Fiji. Avicult. Mag., pp. 164-171.

Ramsay, E. P.
  1864 On the *Didunculus strigirostris* or tooth-billed pigeon from Upolo. Ibis, pp. 98-100.
  1876 Description of a new species of the genus *Lamprolia* Finsch from Fiji; *Lamprolia klinesmithi*, sp. nov. Proc. Linn. Soc. New South Wales, 1:68-69.
  1876 Remarks on a collection of birds lately received from Fiji,

with a list of all species at present known to inhabit the Fiji Islands. Proc. Lin. Soc. New South Wales, 1:69-80.

1878 Notes on some birds from Savage Island, Tutuila, etc., in the collection of the Rev. Mr. Whitmee, FRGS etc. Proc. Linn. Soc. New South Wales, 2:139.

Reichenow, A.

1891 Uber eine Vogelsammlung von den Fidschi—Inseln. Journ. f. Orn., 39:126-130.

Ripley, D., and H. Birckhead

1942 Birds collected during the Whitney South Sea Expedition, LI. Am. Mus. Novit., 1192:1-14.

Sachet, M. H.

1954 A summary of information on Rose Atoll. Atoll Research Bulletin, 29:1-25.

Salvadori, T.

1877 Notes on two birds from the Fiji Islands. Ibis, p. 142-144.

Schwartz, C. W., and E. R. Schwartz

1951 Food habits of the barred dove in Hawaii. Wilson Bull., 63:149-156.

Shorthouse, J. F.

1967 Notes on seabirds on Vatu Ira Island, Fiji—Sept. 1966. Sea Swallow, 19:35-38.

Sibson, R. B.

1965 A note on wandering tattlers in Fiji. Notornis, 12:248-250.

Slater, P.

1971 A Field guide to Australian birds, Non-passerines, pp. 1-428.

Smart, J. B.

1971 Notes on the occurrence of waders in Fiji. Notornis, 18:267-279.

Stickney, E. H.

1943 Birds collected during the Whitney South Sea Expedition, LIII. Northern shore birds in the Pacific. Am. Mus. Novit., 1248:1-9.

Townsend, C. H., and A. Wetmore

1919 Reports on the scientific results of the expedition to the Tropical Pacific in charge of Alexander Agassiz, on the U. S. Fish Commission Steamer *Albatross,* from August, 1899 to March, 1900, Commander Jefferson F. Moser,

U.S.N., commanding. Bull. Mus. Comp. Zool.,
63:151–225.

Watling, D.
 1975 Observations on the ecological separation of two intro-
       duced congeneric mynahs (*Acridotheres*) in Fiji. Notornis,
       22:37–53.

Whitmee, S. J.
 1874 Letter to P. L. Sclater on birds of Samoa. Proc. Zool. Soc.
       London, pp. 183–186.
 1875 List of Samoan birds, with notes on their habits. Ibis, pp.
       436–447.
 1876 List of Samoan birds, with notes on their habits. Ibis, pp.
       504–506.

Williams, G. R.
 1960 The birds of Pitcairn Island, Central South Pacific Ocean.
       Ibis, 102:58–70.

Wilson, S. B.
 1907 Notes on birds of Tahiti and the Society Group. Ibis, pp.
       373–379.

Wodizicki, K.
 1971 The birds of Niue Island, South Pacific: an annotated
       checklist. Notornis, 18:291–304.

Wood, C. A.
 1923 The Fijian crimson-breasted parrot. Emu, 23:118–123.
 1924 The golden doves of Fiji. Bird Lore, 26:387–390.

Wood, C. A., and A. Wetmore
 1925 A collection of birds from the Fiji Islands. Ibis, pp.
       814–855.
 1926 A collection of birds from the Fiji Islands, pt. 3. Ibis, pp.
       91–136.

Yaldwin, J. C.
 1952 Notes on the present status of Samoan birds. Notornis,
       5:28–30.

Ziswiler, V.
 1970 Die Bedrohung der Landvogelfauna südwestpazifischer
       Inseln. Zool. Mus. der Univ. Zürich, pp. 1–18.

Ziswiler, V., H. R. Güttinger, and H. Bregulla
 1972 Monographie der Gattung *Erythrura* Swainson, 1837
       (Aves, Passeres, Estrildidae). Bonner Zool. Mono., No. 2,
       pp. 1–158.

LIST of ISLAND NAMES

Here follows a partial list of localities in the South Pacific as cited by the gazetteers of *Official Standard Names Approved by the U.S. Board on Geographic Names,* prepared in the Office of Geography, Department of Interior, Washington, DC. Obsolete names, variant spellings, and common misspellings are listed, followed by their equivalent, correct spelling or name as given in the gazetteers. Names in parentheses indicate the island group in which the locality is found.

Ahe (Tuamotu)
Ahii = Ahe
Ahunui (Tuamotu)
Aisa = Aiwa
Aitutaki (Cook)
Aitutalei = Aitutaki
Aiva = Aiwa
Aiwa (Fiji)
Akiaki (Taumotu)
Alewa Kalon = Yalewa Kalou
Alofa = Alofi
Alofi (Horne)
American Samoa
Anaa (Tuamotu)
Anuu = Aunuu
Apataki (Tuamotu)
Apolima (West. Samoa)
Aratika (Tuamotu)
Arutea = Arutua
Arutua (Tuamotu)
Asawa Ilau (Fiji)
Ata (Tonga)
Atiu (Cook)
Aua = Ava
Aukena (Tuamotu)
Aukina = Aukena
Aunuu (Amer. Samoa)
Austral Islands
Ava (Tonga)
Avea (Fiji)

Beabea = Pepea
Bora-Bora (Society)
Boscawen = Tafahi

Christmas = Christmas Atoll
Christmas Atoll (Line Islands)
Cook Islands

Danger = Danger Atoll
Danger Atoll (Cook)
Dapu (Marquesas)
Ducie

Eiao (Marquesas)
Eiau = Eiao
Eua (Tonga)
Euakafa (Tonga)
Euakapa = Euakafa

Faaite (Tuamotu)
Fagataufau = Ahunui
Faite = Faaite
Fakahigo = Fakahiku
Fakahiku (Tonga)
Fakahina (Tuamotu)
Fakapoio (Tuamotu)
Fakaraua = Fakarava
Fakarava (Tuamotu)
Fannu Lai = Fonualei
Fanua = Fonualei

193

Fanua Lai = Fonualei
Fanuaika = Fonuaika
Fao = Foa
Fatu Hiva (Marquesas)
Fatu Huku (Marquesas)
Fatuhiva = Fatu Hiva
Fatuhuku = Fatu Huku
Fenua Ura = Scilly
Fiji Islands
Foa (Tonga)
Fonifua = Fonoifua
Fonoifra = Fonoifua
Fonoifua (Tonga)
Fonua Lai = Fonualei
Fonuaika (Tonga)
Fonualei (Tonga)
Fortuna = Futuna
Fotuhaa (Tonga)
Fotuna = Futuna
Fua = Foa
Fulanga (Fiji)
Futuna (Horne)

Gasele = Ngasele Bay

Haafeva (Tonga)
Haano (Tonga)
Haapai Group (Tonga)
Had = Hao
Hao (Tuamotu)
Hapai = Haapai Group
Hatutu (Marquesas)
Henderson Island
Hiti (Tuamotu)
Hiuaoa = Hiva Oa
Hiva Oa (Marquesas)
Hivaoa = Hiva Oa
Hivaou = Hiva Oa
Honden = Pukapuka
Honga = Hunga
Honga Hapai = Hunga Haapai
Honga Tonga = Hunga Tonga
Hongahapai = Hunga Haapai
Hongatonga = Hunga Tonga

Hoorn Islands = Horne Islands
Horne Islands
Huaheine = Huahine
Huaheni = Huahine
Huahine (Society)
Huahuna = Ua Huka
Huamiua (Marquesas)
Huapu = Ua Pu
Hunga (Tonga)
Hunga Haapai (Tonga)
Hunga Tonga (Tonga)

Ilau (Fiji)

Kamaka (Tuamotu)
Kambara (Fiji)
Kanathea (Fiji)
Kanathia = Kanathea
Kandavu (Fiji)
Kao (Tonga)
Kapa (Tonga)
Katafanga (Fiji)
Katavanga = Katafanga
Katiu (Tuamotu)
Katui = Katiu
Kauehi (Tuamotu)
Kaukura (Tuamotu)
Kavehi = Kauehi
Kawa-Kawa = Vawa
Kelefesia (Tonga)
Keppel = Niuatoputapu
Keuehi = Kauehi
Kimbombo Islands (Fiji)
Kio (Fiji)
Komo (Fiji)
Koro (Fiji)
Kukulau (Fiji)

Lakemba (Fiji)
Lalona = Telekiaapai
Late (Tonga)
Lau Archipelago (Fiji)
Lauthala (Fiji)
Lefuka = Lifuka

Leleuvia (Fiji)
Levuka = Luvuka
Lifuka (Tonga)
Line Islands
Lua Hoko (Tonga)
Luathala = Lauthala
Luohoko = Lua Hoko
Luvuka (Fiji)

Magareva (Tuamotu)
Maiao (Society)
Maiatho (Fiji)
Maitea = Mehetia
Makaroa (Tuamotu)
Makatea (Tuamotu)
Makemo (Tuamotu)
Makong = Makongai
Makongai (Fiji)
Malake (Fiji)
Malaki = Malake
Malola = Malolo
Malolo (Fiji)
Mana (Fiji)
Mangaia (Cook)
Mangareva = Magareva
Mango (Fiji)
Mania = Mana
Manihi (Tuamotu)
Maninita (Tonga)
Manono (West. Samoa)
Manonoe = Manono
Manoui = Manui
Manua Islands (Amer. Samoa)
Manui (Tuamotu)
Marambo (Fiji)
Maria (Tuamotu)
Marquesas Islands
Marutea (Tuamotu)
Marutua = Marutea
Matahiva (Tuamotu)
Matathawa Levu (Fiji)
Matathoni = Matathawa Levu
Matathoui = Matathawa Levu
Mathuata (Fiji)

Matuka (Fiji)
Matuku (Fiji)
Maturei-Vavao (Tuamotu)
Mauke (Cook)
Maungaone = Moungaone
Maupiti (Society)
Mbatika = Mbatiki
Mbatiki (Fiji)
Mbenga = Mbengga
Mbengga (Fiji)
Mbengha = Mbengga
Mbua Bay (Fiji)
Mbulia (Fiji)
Mehetia (Society)
Mitiaro (Cook)
Moaia = Moala
Moala (Fiji)
Moengava (Fiji)
Mokani (Fiji)
Mokongai (Fiji)
Monuriki (Fiji)
Moorea (Society)
Mopelia (Society)
Motane (Marquesas)
Mothe (Fiji)
Motoateiko = Motu Teiko
Motu Teiko (Tuamotu)
Motuiti (Marquesas)
Mounagaone = Moungaone
Moungaone (Tonga)
Munia (Fiji)
Mureia (Tuamotu)

Naiau = Nayau
Nairai (Fiji)
Naitamba = Naitaumba
Naitaumba (Fiji)
Nakuemanu (Fiji)
Namena = Namenalala
Namenalala (Fiji)
Namuka (Fiji)
Namuka Ilau = Namuka-I-Lau
Namukaiki = Nomuka Iki
Namuka-I-Lau (Fiji)

Namukalau (Fiji)
Namukallau = Namukalau
Nanuku Levu (Fiji)
Napuka (Tuamotu)
Natewa Peninsula (Fiji)
Nathoulla = Nathula
Nathula (Fiji)
Navandra (Fiji)
Naviti (Fiji)
Navua (Fiji)
Nayau (Fiji)
Ndravuni (Fiji)
Ngamea = Nggamea
Ngamia = Nggamea
Ngasele Bay (Fiji)
Ngau (Fiji)
Ngele Levu = Nggele Levu
Nggalito (Fiji)
Nggamea (Fiji)
Nggele Levu (Fiji)
Ngualito = Nggalito
Niaou = Niau
Niau (Tuamotu)
Niaufou = Niuafoo
Nihiru (Tuamotu)
Niuafoo (Tonga)
Niuafou = Niuafoo
Niuatoputapu (Tonga)
Niue
Nivafo'ou = Niuafoo
Nive = Niue
Nomuka (Tonga)
Nomuka Iki (Tonga)
Nomukaiki = Nomuka Iki
Nukahiva = Nuku Hiva
Nuku Hiva (Marquesas)
Nukuhiva = Nuku Hiva
Nukuhivo = Nuku Hiva
Nukuhivu = Nuku Hiva
Nukulau (Fiji)
Nukumbasanga (Fiji)

Oaa = Oua
Oeno

Ofalanga = Ofolanga
Ofolanga (Tonga)
Ofu (Amer. Samoa)
Olorua (Fiji)
Olosega (Amer. Samoa)
Olosenga = Olosega
Olosinga = Olosega
Oneata (Fiji)
Onega = Ongea Levu
Ongea Levu (Fiji)
Ono (Fiji)
Ono Ilau = Ono-I-Lau
Ono-I-Lau (Fiji)
Ono Llau = Ono-I-Lau
Oua (Tonga)
Ovaka (Tonga)
Ovalau (Fiji)

Palmerston Island
Papa (Austral)
Paraoa (Tuamotu)
Pepea (Tonga)
Pinaki (Tuamotu)
Pitcairn Island
Pudupudua = Putuputua
Pukapuka (Tuamotu)
Putuputua (Tonga)

Raevavae (Austral)
Raiatea (Society)
Rambi (Fiji)
Rangiroa (Tuamotu)
Rapa (Austral)
Raraka (Tuamotu)
Raroia (Tuamotu)
Rarotonga (Cook)
Ravaivai = Raevavae
Ravavai = Raevavae
Rewa (Fiji)
Riatea = Raiatea
Rimatara (Austral)
Rimitara = Rimatara
Rimituru = Rimatara
Rose Island (Amer. Samoa)

Rotuma
Rurutu (Austral)

Samoa, American
Samoa, Western
Sandal Wood Bay = Mbua Bay
Savage Island = Niue
Savaii (West. Samoa)
Scilly (Society)
Society Islands
Solomon Islands
Sovu Islets (Fiji)

Taenga (Tuamotu)
Tafahi (Tonga)
Tafalu (Tonga)
Tahaa (Society)
Tahaiti = Tahiti
Tahanea (Tuamotu)
Tahiti (Society)
Tahuata (Marquesas)
Taiaro (Tuamotu)
Takahau (Tuamotu)
Takapoto (Tuamotu)
Takaroa (Tuamotu)
Takume (Tuamotu)
Takurea = Takume
Tau (Amer. Samoa)
Taveuni (Fiji)
Taviuni = Taveuni
Tavua (Fiji)
Tavunasithe = Tavunasithi
Tavunasithi (Fiji)
Tavutha (Fiji)
Teauba = Teaupa
Teaupa (Tonga)
Telekiaapai (Tonga)
Telekitonga (Tonga)
Telekivavau (Tonga)
Temoe (Tuamotu)
Tenaranga = Tenaruga
Tenarare = Tenararo
Tenararo (Tuamotu)
Tenaruga (Tuamotu)

Tenarunga = Tenaruga
Tenerunga = Tenaruga
Tepato = Tepoto
Tepoto (Tuamotu)
Tetiaroa (Society)
Thakaundrove Peninsula =
    Natewa Peninsula
Thikombia (Fiji)
Thikombia Ilau =
    Thikombia-I-Lau
Thikombia-I-Lau (Fiji)
Thithia (Fiji)
Thithial = Thithia
Thombia (Fiji)
Tickahau = Tikehau
Tikahao = Tikehau
Tikahau = Tikehau
Tikehau (Tuamotu)
Tikei (Tuamotu)
Timoe Atoll (Tuamotu)
Toao = Toau
Toau (Tuamotu)
Tofanga = Tofonga
Tofonga (Tonga)
Tofua (Tonga)
Toku (Tonga)
Tokulu (Tonga)
Tolanga = Tofonga
Tomberua (Fiji)
Tonga
Tongatabu = Tongatapu
Tongatapu (Tonga)
Tongua = Tungua
Tonumea (Tonga)
Tonumeia = Tonumea
Tonunieia = Tonumea
Totoya (Fiji)
Tuamotu Archipelago
Tuanake (Tuamotu)
Tubuai (Austral)
Tuku I = Toku
Tungua (Tonga)
Tureia (Tuamotu)
Turtle Island = Vatoa

Tutuila (Amer. Samoa)
Tuvatha = Tuvutha
Tuvutha (Fiji)

Ua Huka (Marquesas)
Ua Pu (Marquesas)
Uahuka = Ua Huka
Uanukuhahaki = Uonuku Hahake
Uanukuhilifu = Uonuku Hihifo
Uea (Fiji)
Uia = Uiha
Uiha (Tonga)
Unanukuhalaki = Uonuku
  Hahake
Uoleva (Tonga)
Uonuku Hahake (Tonga)
Uonuku Hihifo (Tonga)
Upolu (West. Samoa)
Urha = Uiha
Uvea (Horne)

Vahaga (Tuamotu)
Vahanga = Vahaga
Vanavana (Tuamotu)
Vanevana = Vanavana
Vanua Kula (Fiji)
Vanua Levu (Fiji)
Vanua Masi = Vanuamasi
Vanua Mbaiavu = Vanuambalavu
Vanua Mbalavu = Vanuambalavu
Vanua Vatu = Vanuavatu
Vanuamasi (Fiji)
Vanuambalavu (Fiji)
Vanuavatu (Fiji)
Varitao (Austral)
Vatanua (Fiji)
Vatoa (Fiji)
Vatu Ira = Vatu-I-Ra
Vatu Leile = Vatulele
Vatu Vara = Vatuvara
Vatu-I-Ra (Fiji)
Vatulele (Fiji)
Vatuvara (Fiji)
Vavau (Tonga)

Vavitao = Raevavae
Vawa (Fiji)
Vita Levu = Viti Levu
Viti Levu (Fiji)
Viwa (Fiji)
Voini (Fiji)
Vomo (Fiji)
Vormo = Vomo
Vuro (Fiji)

Waia = Waya
Wailangilala = Welangilala
Wakaia = Wakaya
Wakaya (Fiji)
Wallis Island
Wangava = Wanggava
Wanggava (Fiji)
Watanua (Fiji)
Waya (Fiji)
Welangilala (Fini)
Western Samoa

Yalewa Kalou (Fiji)
Yandua (Fiji)
Yanganga = Yangganga
Yangasa Cluster = Yangasalevu
Yangasalevu (Fiji)
Yangganga (Fiji)
Yankeve = Yaukuve Levu
Yankuve = Yaukuve Levu
Yanuaya = Yanuya
Yanutha (Fiji)
Yanuya (Fiji)
Yasawa (Fiji)
Yathata (Fiji)
Yaukuve Lailai (Fiji)
Yaukuve Levu (Fiji)
Yendua = Yandua

INDEX

199

LINE ISLANDS

Nu

Vostok °o
Island

°Caroline Island

°Flint
Island

Takaroa

TUAMO

Rangiroa

Makatea

Huahine

Bora-Bora

Tahaa

Apataki
Raraka

Raiatea

Fakarava

Tetiaroa

Moorea

Anaa

Hi

Tahiti

Mehetia

SOCIETY ISLANDS

ro

uke

Duke of Gloucester
Islands

Tematangio

°Maria

Mur

Rimatara°

°Rururu

Tubuai

Raevavae

AUSTRAL ISLANDS

Rapa°

Bass Islands